HAMPSHIRE
HEADLINES
JOHN BARTON

HAMPSHIRE
HEADLINES

★

JOHN BARTON

COUNTRYSIDE BOOKS
NEWBURY, BERKSHIRE

First Published 1993
© John Barton 1993

COUNTRYSIDE BOOKS
3 Catherine Road
Newbury, Berkshire

ISBN 1 85306 268 5

Cover Design by Mon Mohan

Produced through MRM Associates Ltd., Reading
Typeset by Paragon Typesetters, Queensferry, Clwyd
Printed in England

To Charlie

Contents

Foreword

★

All the events described in this book were the subject of headline stories in the national and local newspapers. They all without exception aroused great public interest at the time. It is tempting to speculate whether they would receive the same news coverage or provoke the same interest today. The Farnborough air disaster and the Schneider Trophy undoubtedly would but others, such as the prize-fight and the Southampton murder, might not.

I should like to thank the staff of the Local Studies Libraries at Farnborough, Portsmouth, Southampton and Winchester for their help in locating information, the Hampshire Chronicle, Southern Evening Echo and Portsmouth Publishing and Printing for permission to quote news reports and headlines, and not least Countryside Books for their encouragement and helpful suggestions relating to the contents of the book.

The photographs are reproduced by permission of Hampshire County Library (Winchester diver and King's House), Portsmouth City Records Office (1891 blizzard), Aldershot News Group (Cody's crash), and the Salvation Army. The photograph of the Supermarine S6A is reproduced by kind permission of the RAF Museum at Hendon (Schneider Trophy). The photograph of Portsmouth Football team was taken by Steven Cribb and is reproduced by kind permission of Mick Cooper.

John Barton
August 1993

Captain Swing's
Last Victim

★

In Micheldever churchyard there is a grave on which, it is said, the snow never lies. Buried there is Henry Cook, an illiterate farm labourer who was only 19 years old when he was swept up in a desperate struggle on the part of the rural poor to improve their lot, only to end on the gallows. His death was just part of the price paid by the labourers for their acts of violence and destruction that in the end gained them very little.

In 1830 the standard of living of English farm labourers was lower than it had ever been; they were as poor as any workers in Europe. Whereas their fathers and grandfathers had enjoyed meat, cheese and bacon, they and their families subsisted largely on bread and potatoes. Prisoners were no worse off than farm labourers, whose weekly wage of about nine shillings was not the minimum on which a family could live but the wage that employers thought would prevent another Peasants' Revolt.

The main cause of their plight was the adoption of the 'Speenhamland' system devised by Berkshire justices in Speenhamland, Newbury, in 1795, ruling that wages should be subsidized out of the local rates. This system for 40 years proved to be an unmitigated disaster for the rural population as it encouraged farmers to pay as little as possible, knowing that the rates would bring the wages up to subsistence level but no more. Labourers on the other hand had no reason to work hard, as no effort on their part would earn them any more than a subsistence wage.

Farm labourers had no trade union and few friends to help them. Landowners, aristocracy and government treated them with indifference and contempt. One forthright champion was William Cobbett, who in such works as *Rural Rides* eloquently described the pitiful state of poverty and degradation into which the English farm labourers had sunk.

Farmers were often willing to increase wages on condition that the clergy reduced their tithes; a marked feature of the troubles that erupted was the alliance of farmer and worker against the parson. The workers tried to eke out a living by poaching, thieving and smuggling, but as the penalty for those activities was execution or transportation, many thousands of good men were summarily banished to the other side of the world. In short, the English farm labourers were desperate, and became even more so when the increasing use of threshing-machines threatened their livelihood.

At first there were threatening letters, sent to farmers and landowners, originally anonymous but later signed by a fictitious 'Captain Swing'. The first 'Swing' letter appeared in *The Times* in October 1830 and the name was then used all over the country. The instigators of the riots that were to come thus acquired the collective nickname of 'Captain Swing'.

The violence began in Kent where on 1st June 1830 hayricks and a barn were set on fire at Orpington, then on 28th August the first threshing-machine was destroyed near Canterbury. The riots spread throughout Kent and Surrey and arson continued for several weeks, but it was in Hampshire and Wiltshire that the rebellion became most widespread and serious. In Hampshire the riots, although short-lived (two weeks in November), resulted in much damage to farm property and the destruction of two workhouses. There was less arson but more machine-breaking than in Kent and Surrey.

On Thursday 18th November at Overton several hundred

labourers thronged the streets, many of them demanding food and money from the terrified inhabitants. The farmers who employed them rode into the village and successfully pacified and dispersed them by promising higher wages. Early the next day the labourers again assembled in the streets, this time armed with sticks and clubs, declaring angrily that they were not satisfied with the promises made the previous day. Violence was averted by the arrival of Henry Hunt, one of the leaders of the radical group dedicated to parliamentary reform and social change. He agreed to arbitrate between the two sides, and suggested that wages should be raised from nine to 12 shillings a week and that the rents of the workers' houses should be paid by the employers. This was agreed by both sides and within ten minutes the market place was empty, the men having immediately returned to work.

At Barton Stacey, between Winchester and Andover, money was demanded from the curate before three large barns and other buildings were destroyed. A mob of over 700 labourers invaded the villages around Micheldever and in spite of a promise of an increase in wages, destroyed all the threshing machines they could find. No trouble was recorded from Basingstoke, though the *Hampshire Chronicle* reported that ladies there were alarmed lest the mob should 'pay them a visit'.

Some of this mob marched to The Grange at Northington, home of the Barings, the millionaire bankers. During a violent confrontation at Northington Down Farm a sledge-hammer blow was aimed at William Baring by young Henry Cook. Baring's hat was knocked off and he fell to the ground but suffered no serious injury, except to his dignity. Cook was arrested some days later and charged with attempted murder. As a result of this riot, troops were summoned from Portsmouth to restore order.

Between Sutton Scotney and Stratton the same day the Reverend Dr Newbolt, a county magistrate, met a large mob armed with sledge-hammers, saws, axes and sticks. In an effort to placate them he avowed that he had 'always been their friend and ever would be'. He said that their demand for a wage of 12 shillings a week was very reasonable and he would recommend it to their employers.

The riots at Andover, which lasted for several days, began with the destruction of a threshing-machine. One of the ringleaders was thrown into gaol, only to be rescued immediately by a mob who forced open the gaol doors and carried him in triumph through the streets. Andover was said to be more like a 'besieged place' than a country town. On Saturday 20th November a crowd that marched to Tasker's Waterloo Ironworks at Upper Clatford destroyed all the machinery they could lay their hands on, and damaged a water-wheel and some buildings. At the subsequent trial of the ringleaders, Robert Tasker, who sympathized with their demands if not with their actions, refused to identify any particular individuals and made light of the damage, but this did not prevent them from being sentenced to transportation.

On Sunday 21st November a mob demanding food and money broke into several houses and inns west of Winchester, including Houghton Mill, Bossington House, the King's Arms at Stockbridge and Rookley House at King's Somborne. The next day at Stockbridge vicarage they demanded a reduction in tithes, and also sovereigns equal in number to the 21 years the vicar had been there, threatening to set fire to the house unless he complied.

Many confrontations occurred between magistrates and constables on the one hand and labourers and their supporters on the other, some ending amicably and others in a riot. One such meeting at the Anchor Inn at Liphook on Monday 22nd November could have resulted in violence but for the decisive action of Dr Quarrier, a county magistrate. He identified the ringleader of the mob as Thomas Hamblin, a stranger to the area, and had him arrested on the spot by a constable and sent by coach to Portsmouth gaol. Another gathering of workers the next day at Steep churchyard was also dispersed by Dr Quarrier, who promised to use his influence with the farmers. He then went to Portsmouth to ask for soldiers to be sent to Petersfield to quell an expected disturbance on market day. If all local magistrates had taken similar firm action to check disorderly meetings before they got out of hand many of the acts of violence and destruction would have been averted.

On this Monday of violence a mob of 300 labourers went to Selborne workhouse and politely told the wife of the master (who was away) to leave the building. They removed the roof, broke the doors and windows and set fire to the furniture. After that they went to the vicar and so frightened him that he agreed to reduce his tithes from £600 to £300 a year. The following day they went to Headley, extracted a similar promise from the vicar there and destroyed the workhouse, leaving only the sick ward standing. 'Not a room was left entire', said the workhouse master at the subsequent trial. (It was rebuilt and is now a private house.)

The Selborne mob had been summoned by a horn blown by John Newland, now known as 'The Trumpeter'. After the riots he hid for some time on Selborne Hanger but was eventually captured and sentenced to six months hard labour. He died in 1868 and his grave in Selborne churchyard is marked by a stone inscribed simply 'The Trumpeter'.

At Itchen Abbas that same Monday a pitched battle took place between a mob of 300 labourers and 100 local inhabitants, sworn in as special constables in order to guard Avington House. As a result about 50 of the rioters were taken into custody and 29 were sent to gaol.

One of the last areas in Hampshire to suffer the riots was around the New Forest. At Fordingbridge the rioters were organized by 'Captain Hunt', who rode a white horse. An ostler from Wiltshire whose real name was James Cooper, he and Henry Cook were the only two local men executed for their part in the riots. After destroying all the threshing-machines in the area 300 men marched into Fordingbridge and destroyed the machinery at two mills.

In Southampton the worst outrage was the destruction of Charles Baker's sawmills. Prior warnings resulted in a night patrol of two men and a boy. In spite of this precaution at about 1.30am on Wednesday 22nd November the patrol saw flames in the corner of the building nearest the road. Within half an hour the entire mills were ablaze. The flames, which rose to a great height, were said to have been visible from Farnham in Surrey and from HMS *St Vincent* at Portsmouth. The naval authorities at Portsmouth, believing the fire to be at Fareham, dispatched about 100 marines and sailors to help. Most of them got lost and only a quarter of them arrived at Southampton. The damage to the sawmills amounted to £7,000 and had the opposite effect of that intended by the arsonists – because the installation of the sawmill machinery had not deprived anyone of work but its destruction certainly did.

Overnight fires at Gosport and Wallington caused great alarm. Horse and foot patrols were introduced and farmers kept a nightly watch on their properties. At Fawley about 350 of the 'lower orders' gathered, carrying sticks and 'presenting a formidable appearance'. The magistrates promised to submit their demands to the farmers and give them a reply the next day. In the absence of an immediate reply a riot quickly followed; soldiers charged the mob and took three ringleaders for trial.

On 25th November the Lord Lieutenant of Hampshire (the Duke of Wellington) and the county magistrates issued a number of resolutions to the effect that the uprisings should be suppressed and called on all 'respectable' inhabitants to resist the lawbreakers.

Most landowners and employers in Hampshire agreed to the demand for higher wages, but at Titchfield a resolution

14

was passed expressing regret at not being able to afford to do so and condemning the paying of wages partly out of the poor rate.

By the end of November all was quiet again and the agricultural labourers had returned to work. Had they achieved their ends? For a time they enjoyed improved wages and conditions but after a few years wages fell to their old level. One thing is certain – threshing-machines were not used again for a long time.

At a Special Commission, held in Winchester on 18th December, 285 prisoners were committed for trial, mostly for extorting money and breaking machinery – surprisingly, not a single case of arson. Of 156 liable for the death penalty only two were executed, James Cooper and Henry Cook. After the trials, petitions for reprieve were sent to the Home Office by the people of Gosport, Basingstoke, Portsmouth, Romsey, Whitchurch and Winchester. The Winchester petition for mercy was signed by bankers, Low Church ministers and every tradesman in the city, but not by the cathedral clergy.

Reprieve came, but not for James Cooper and Henry Cook, who were executed on 15th January 1831 at Winchester gaol – Cook for his attack on the son of a wealthy, influential family and Cooper because he had become almost a folk hero and as such was too much of a threat to be left alive. All the prisoners, 150 of whom were at the time still under sentence of death, were forced to witness the executions. Instead of the hundreds of people who usually turned up on these occasions there was only a handful of spectators, mostly young men and boys and a few women, to witness Henry Cook sobbing pitifully as he went to his death. 'Captain Swing' had gathered his last victim.

The Andover Workhouse Scandal

★

In the summer of 1845 alarming rumours began to circulate in the county about the conditions in Andover workhouse. The rumours were based on allegations made by inmates who had recently left the workhouse. The most disturbing of these was that inmates who had the task of grinding bones in the yard were eating the rotten flesh from them because of their hunger.

It was these disclosures that were to bring about the eventual downfall of the Poor Law Commission, and so change attitudes to the destitute poor.

Before the Poor Law Act of 1834 was introduced, the poor people of a parish received an allowance from the local rates, a system under which they were sometimes treated with sympathy and humanity. By 1831 the population of England and Wales had risen to about 14 million (living in two and a half million houses), of whom a great many were classed as poor. Worried about the ever-increasing cost of the rates, the Government passed an act for the building of workhouses throughout the country to be administered by a Poor Law Commission. The poor would not be forced to enter a workhouse as it would be a purely voluntary choice, and once inside they could leave whenever they chose to do so. In the workhouse they would be given food, clothing and medical attention. Those who chose not to become inmates could stay at home and take a chance of finding work. But if they did not find it they would starve.

It was thought that workhouses would cost less than the

existing distribution of bread to the poor, on the supposition that able-bodied idlers who exploited the relief system would not be prepared to enter a workhouse. In fact many workhouses became places of cruelty, deprivation, humiliation and squalor. The very mention of the name filled the poor people in this country with dread until well into the 20th century.

There were at least two influential and outspoken opponents of the workhouse system. One was John Walter, the owner of *The Times* newspaper, and the other was William Cobbett, Member of Parliament, journalist and fearless champion of the poor. For 13 years Walter took every opportunity to highlight the deficiencies of the workhouse system in the columns of his newspaper. Day after day his reports and editorials condemned the workhouses but the authorities ignored all criticism.

Indeed throughout the early years of the workhouse system it seemed that nothing could arouse the public's conscience. *The Times* unfailingly reported in detail every abuse of the system, such as separation of husbands from wives and of children from parents, meagre rations and hard labour. The public was not interested – it enjoyed the 20 per cent reduction in the poor rate at a time, the depression of the early 1840s, when the workhouses were filled to capacity because there was no work available for those who were unemployed.

The harsh workhouse orders and regulations included the following:

'All paupers except the sick, aged, infirm and young children shall rise, be set to work, leave off work and go to bed at specified times [rise 6 am in summer – work for ten hours, 7 am in winter – work for nine hours, to bed 8 pm].

Boys and girls shall be instructed for three hours every day in reading, writing and the Christian religion and receive such other instructions as are calculated to train them in habits of usefulness, industry and virtue.

17

The diet of the paupers shall in no case exceed in quantity and quality the ordinary diet of able-bodied labourers living within the same district.

Any pauper may quit the workhouse upon giving three hours notice to the master, but no able-bodied pauper may quit without also removing the whole of his or her family.

A pauper shall not use obscene or profane language, insult or revile any other pauper or the master or matron, neglect or refuse to work, pretend sickness, be guilty of any act of drunkenness or indecency, and fail to cleanse his or her person.'

Walter's long campaign came to a successful conclusion in 1847 with the abolition of the Poor Law Commission. This itself was a result of the disclosure of the revolting state of affairs at Andover workhouse, which *The Times* had reported in such detail in 1845. A public inquiry at Andover into the misdeeds of those who administered the workhouse there had revealed such a horrifying tale that a Parliamentary Select Committee of Inquiry had followed. This in turn confirmed the findings of the local inquiry and virtually sealed the fate of the Poor Law Commission.

Andover workhouse was built in 1836 and opened its doors on 25th March 1837 to 111 paupers. The chairman of the Board of Guardians was the Reverend Christopher Dodson, who held the post for 40 years. Although a Church of England clergyman he interpreted Christian doctrine according to the Victorian opinion that rich and poor were allotted their station in life by God. He therefore treated the workhouse poor with unmitigated severity.

Dodson's treatment of the paupers was matched by that of the workhouse governor, ex-Sergeant-Major Colin McDougal, a strict disciplinarian. The latter needed little persuasion by Dodson to adopt a tyrannical and cruel attitude to them. The combination of these two men eventually made life at Andover almost intolerably miserable for the paupers; they left the workhouse if they were fit

The former workhouse at Andover; a public inquiry revealed that the paupers there were so hungry they were scavenging from the animal bones that they had been set to grind.

enough, even although the prospects in the world outside were bleak.

Dodson and his wife, who was the workhouse matron, were in the habit of stealing the inmates' food, meagre though that was and less than the rations in other workhouses. According to the diet sheet of December 1845, breakfast for men consisted of seven ounces of bread and two pints of gruel, dinner twelve ounces of suet pudding or seven ounces of bread and two ounces of cheese, and supper seven ounces of bread and one and a half ounces of cheese. Rations for women were slightly less. Occasionally meat and vegetables were served for dinner. McDougal and his wife each received three times the ration of a pauper but that did not stop them from stealing the children's milk and the beer and gin that the doctor had prescribed for the old and sick inmates.

In order to live up to its name of 'workhouse' inmates were called upon to perform certain tasks, and at Andover all fit men were set to grind animal bones to a powder for use as fertilizer, each man working for such time as it took to grind one hundredweight of bones. The grinding was done with an iron bar weighing 20-30 pounds. Small boys had to work in pairs. The smell from the stinking bones was awful, and the flying fragments of bone chipped and scarred the workers' faces. No wonder many inmates left the workhouse to face possible starvation outside rather than endure this terrible task. Some men ate the marrow from the inside of the bones, saying that it was cleaner than the meat on the outside, and one man admitted to eating raw horse flesh from the bones.

Hugh Mundy, the only one of the guardians with a spark of humanity, decided to find out the truth for himself. He was told by the workers in the yard that the rumours were true; they *were* stealing the bones and gnawing the flesh from them. Knowing he would get nowhere with Dodson and McDougal, Mundy reported the facts to his Member of Parliament, who in turn told John Wakley, Member for Finsbury and friend of Cobbett.

When the matter was raised in the House of Commons the Home Secretary dismissed the story as absurd but nevertheless sent Assistant Poor Law Commissioner Parker to investigate. As a result of the latter's report a public inquiry was ordered, at which the whole terrible story became known. *The Times* reported the proceedings of the inquiry in detail every day; it was just what John Walter had been waiting for all these years. The wave of horror and disgust that followed quickly forced the Government to appoint a Select Committee of Inquiry.

At both the local inquiry and the Select Committee of Inquiry more startling revelations came to light. The Andover guardians were shown to be completely apathetic and not the slightest bit interested in the conditions at the workhouse. Dodson, their chairman, had not visited parts of the workhouse at all during the five years before the inquiries nor had he acquainted himself with the Commissioners' regulations for the last three years.

The workhouse doctor had been well aware of the brutality meted out to the inmates but had been afraid to complain to the guardians in case he got the sack. It was also revealed that between 1837 and 1846 61 inmates of Andover were sent to prison for various offences, some no doubt because they knew that food and discipline in prison were certainly no worse than in the workhouse.

The children in the workhouse were caned on the slightest excuse by McDougal, and by his son and daughter who gave them lessons. (What they taught is not recorded.) If the older children ran away they were flogged when they were caught. One three year old boy, Jimmy Brown, was caned so hard by McDougal that the cane broke across his back. For this McDougal was sued for assault by the boy's father and fined one shilling and costs.

A girl named Hannah Joyce had a five week old baby, which died suddenly one night. Because the child was illegitimate she was ordered to spend the night in the mortuary with the dead child; when she refused she was locked in an empty bedroom. Next day she was ordered to carry the tiny coffin through the streets of Andover to the cemetery. When Hannah left the workhouse a week later she had to endure a noisy and degrading parade through the ranks of the other inmates with Dodson and McDougal laughing at the spectacle from the boardroom window.

McDougal himself was not averse to sleeping with any of the female inmates who would let him do so, usually in return for extra food and drink. They were always too afraid to tell Mrs McDougal about her husband's behaviour.

One of the recommendations of the Select Committee was that 'the crushing of bones or any labour of a penal or disgusting nature should not be adopted by boards of guardians, as such a course must tend to prevent the really destitute poor from entering the union house, and is not consistent with a mild and considerate administration of the law.'

The Committee also criticised Assistant Commissioner Parker for conducting the public inquiry at Andover in a rude and partial manner, interrupting witnesses and excusing McDougal's actions at every opportunity. The Commissioners, with *The Times* and public opinion against them, had asked Parker to resign after the inquiries. They now decided that perhaps he had been hard done by, but it was too late to make amends because the Poor Law Commission itself was abolished in July 1847, although workhouses continued to function as homes for the poor and needy until midway through the 20th century.

The guardians never forgave the inmates for exposing them to public condemnation and ridicule and after the inquiries they made life at the workhouse even more miserable. The grinding of bones was discontinued but the breaking of flints took its place, which was even worse in a way because they could not alleviate the paupers' hunger! Conditions certainly became worse and were not helped by the fact that Dodson's resignation was not accepted. He continued as chairman of the guardians for another 30 years. But Andover was not typical of workhouses in general – it was an example of uncontrolled local administration.

The workhouse always had an evil reputation, but it was not universally deserved – there were good workhouses as well as ones like Andover.

The inmate of a workhouse was not necessarily worse off in terms of material comfort than a person living at home on poor relief. People on relief lost their status as citizens and their right to vote anyway, but the main difference was that workhouse inmates lost their independence. The workhouse was the first experiment in state institutional care; it served as a school, asylum, hospital and old people's home. But the system was bound to fail because there was no easy way of deterring the able-bodied from seeking admission while at the same time encouraging the sick and helpless to do so and it was based on an indefensible assumption – that poverty was due to idleness and that paupers were little more than criminals deserving only to be locked up.

The Great Prize-fight

★

At 4 am on Tuesday 17th April 1860 two trains left London Bridge station, their carriages packed to capacity. The passengers were predominantly upper and middle class, but with a fair number of the 'lower orders' as they were then termed. Lords, baronets, Members of Parliament and journalists sat with tradesmen and workers all with a common purpose. As the trains rattled on through south London and Surrey small groups of policemen waited at stations along the line to put a halt to the affair, but at Reigate the trains unexpectedly turned off the main Brighton line towards Guildford, thus evading them. Three hours after leaving London the trains stopped at the London and South Eastern's small station at Farnborough (now Farnborough North) in Hampshire.

As the passengers alighted they looked around for Tom Oliver, the organizer of the trip, but he was already running across the marshy fields towards the Blackwater River, which here forms the boundary between Hampshire and Surrey. The motley crowd hurried after him as he leapt ditches and scrambled through hedges. Many of them were not used to this exercise and fell into the waist-high ditch-water.

When news of this extraordinary invasion reached the inhabitants of Farnborough village they locked themselves indoors and left their part-time constable to investigate. He hastened to the scene; the trains standing at the station and the huge crowd surrounding a roped-off square of turf near the river confirmed his suspicions. There was obviously going to be a prize-fight.

He was right – it was to be the most famous fight yet held

in England, a fight that had gripped the public's imagination ever since it had been announced. Because of its cruelty and vulgarity prize-fighting was increasingly under attack by many people at that time and although it was not illegal, its promoters were often prosecuted for causing a breach of the peace.

It was not until 1867 that the Queensberry rules were introduced into prize-fighting, decreeing the use of boxing-gloves and limiting the rounds to three minutes with one-minute intervals. But in 1860 the rules were still primitive – bare fists and the round to end only when one boxer was knocked or thrown down, when he was allowed 30 seconds to get to the centre-mark again (hence the expression 'up to scratch').

Tom Sayers had been the acknowledged champion of England since 1857, and as such was obliged to accept a challenge from anyone during the three years that he held the 'belt'. A former bricklayer, now an innkeeper, he weighed only eleven stone and was only five feet eight and a half inches tall, but he was very tough, and a clever and crafty fighter. Even so he seemed no match for his opponent, the American John Heenan, 13½ stone and nearly five inches taller than Sayers and broad in proportion.

The two men, who had never met before, shook hands. Heenan won the toss for corners and chose to have his back to the sun. At 7.30 am the fight began. In the first two rounds they sparred warily but Sayers drew first blood with a punch to Heenan's face. In the next round Sayers received a blow that sent him reeling, and after trying to get in close to Heenan got a punch to the forehead that knocked him into his corner. Sayers was having trouble with the sun in his eyes and in the next round a mighty punch floored him again. He now realised that it was useless to swap punches at arm's length with a man of Heenan's strength and reach, so he tried again to get in close to his opponent, only to be sent staggering from another hefty blow.

In the next round the two men feinted and sparred so long and so cautiously that eventually they both lowered their arms and laughed – for the last time; the fight now developed into a merciless exchange of punches. For the fourth time Sayers was knocked down and in his corner cold sponges were pressed to his bruises. Already with only a few rounds gone the spectators were taunting him, saying that he was virtually finished and was no match for his powerful opponent. Sayers heard these comments and it seemed to mark a turning-point in the fight.

At the start of the next round Sayers evaded an enormous punch that would probably have knocked him out, and before Heenan could recover landed a fierce punch on his right eye, which cut open the American's cheek and sent him reeling. Sayers followed this up with two more hard blows to the face; Heenan's features soon became unrecognizable beneath the blood and bruises. But Sayers had not got off scot-free. A tremendous blow on his right arm had probably broken a bone, because the arm soon began to swell and proved so painful that it was practically useless for the rest of the contest, and he had to fight on with only one good arm. He made effective use of this, however, and landed another terrible blow on Heenan's face. While it was being sponged Sayers went over to his opponent's corner to inspect the damage – and presumably to see how he could make it worse. In the next round the American landed a punch on Sayers's nose that was heard by the whole crowd. At the end of this round, which lasted 13 minutes, both men had to be carried to their corners.

In the next round Sayers delivered four successive punches on Heenan and, had he the use of his right arm, might well have finished him off. But he dare not get in too close to his opponent and finished the round with a blow to Heenan's ribs that sounded, wrote the *Hampshire Chronicle*, 'as if a box had been smashed in', and another to his face so violent that it covered Heenan in blood and sent Sayers

26

himself reeling from the force of the blow. Now they went for each other hammer and tongs, the round ending with Sayers knocked down. Both men were now very much the worse for wear and obviously distressed. Heenan especially was a pitiful sight; his face was gashed with deep wounds, the right side of it beaten to a pulp.

When they came out again Heenan knocked Sayers down with a tremendous punch, and in the following round lifted him easily and threw him heavily to the ground. In the next round Sayers hit Heenan on the left and only good eye. In return Heenan floored Sayers, who bounced back in the next round with a blow to Heenan's face that was heard all over the field, and then for the one and only time in the contest threw Heenan down.

In the next two rounds Sayers was hit several times and appeared to be stunned, yet at the start of the following round came out apparently quite fresh, not nearly as bloodstained as Heenan, who according to the *Hampshire Chronicle* was 'a disgusting object'. In the next few rounds each boxer gave as good as he got, but Heenan's left eye was rapidly becoming as useless as his right.

In the 38th round Heenan trapped Sayers's head under his left arm and held him down. Sayers managed to give Heenan two punches to the face with his left arm but Heenan then got Sayers's neck over the rope and leant his whole weight on it. Sayers began to turn black in the face and undoubtedly would have been strangled had not the rules, such as they were, provided for such an eventuality. The two umpires called for the ropes to be cut and both boxers slumped to the ground, Sayers half-strangled.

The police force, summoned by the local constable, had arrived some time ago but had been unable to penetrate the dense crowd of spectators. They made a determined effort to get through to the ring, but the spectators were equally determined to keep them out. When the ropes were cut the ring was invaded by rival supporters and the two boxers scarcely had room to manoeuvre. The umpires and referee lost control of the fight but the spectators in the ring allowed fair play as far as possible. Four more rounds were fought, bringing the total to 42, each man landing savage blows on the other.

Heenan was by now virtually blind and, lunging in desperation in the direction of Sayers, succeeded only in knocking one of his opponent's seconds head over heels. When the police at last got into the ring the referee immediately halted the contest. Both men appeared to be quite willing to end it. Sayers walked away with his right arm helpless by his side, his head and face in a sorry state. Heenan also walked away and even jumped the ditches, but he was so blind that he had to be led to the train.

How much longer the fight would have continued had the police not intervened nobody knows, but unless Heenan had been able to land a knock-out blow before he completely lost his sight Sayers would inevitably have finished him off. That Sayers lasted over two hours with only one good arm says much for his stamina and skill and the power of his left arm. Equally Heenan displayed great strength and courage in fighting on with his face in such a state. Nevertheless there is no doubt that it was a sickening spectacle, beside which today's championship fights would look quite gentle affairs.

The editor of *Bell's Life* said that it was the best championship fight ever witnessed, but after praising the skill of both men he criticized Heenan for knocking down Sayers' second. He was of the opinion that Sayers would have won had the fight been allowed to continue.

The referee afterwards declared that he had stopped the fight in response to pleas from Heenan's supporters, who claimed that once the ring was broken, the fight was at an end. Sayers's supporters on the other hand thought that their man would undoubtedly have won in the end. Sayers himself asserted that he would have won in another ten minutes but could have continued if necessary for another hour, and strongly objected to the official decision to call the contest a draw. The famous novelist William Thackeray, who was almost certainly at the fight, said that 'the advantage was all on Sayers' side'. Charles Dickens had intended to go to the contest but at the last moment changed his mind.

Both men wanted to fight again, but their supporters seemed quite happy with the official result. As the police threatened to arrest Sayers and Heenan should they attempt to stage another fight, all such plans were dropped. The prize of £200 was withheld, but Sayers later received a testimonial of £3,000. He had captured the imagination of the British public, and many people who had previously classed prize-fighters with common criminals were enthusiastic in their hero-worship. Even Princess Mary asked for Sayers to be presented to her. But condemnation of such contests was becoming widespread and questions were asked in Parliament.

In retrospect the fight was increasingly seen for what it really was – a disgusting spectacle of human brutality watched by people from all walks of life who in former times had enjoyed such bloodthirsty contests as cock-fighting and bear-baiting. The prize-fighters paid a high price for their fame. Five years later Sayers died of diabetes at the age of 39, all his money gone. Heenan also died before he was 40.

Sweet Fanny Adams

★

'Killed a young girl. It was fine and hot.' This diary entry helped to hang the man responsible for one of the most horrific crimes in Victorian England, an age of many sensational murders but few more revolting.

Alton in 1867 was a quiet little country market town, where nothing very exciting had happened since the Civil War, when Parliamentarians fought their way into the parish church and massacred the Royalist troops sheltering there. Eight-year-old Fanny Adams and her young sister Elizabeth, the children of a bricklayer, lived in Tanhouse Lane, which was then a street of small terraced houses running from Amery Street to the fields west of the town.

On the afternoon of Saturday 24th August, a hot sunny day, they set off with their friend Minnie Warner to play in nearby Flood Meadow. There they met Frederick Baker − a 29 year old Alton solicitor's clerk − dressed in his usual black coat and tall black hat. He followed the girls into the field and picked some berries for them, then gave Elizabeth and Minnie a halfpenny each to buy sweets. When he offered Fanny a halfpenny to go with him across the field she took the money but then refused, so he picked up the crying child and carried her away.

When Elizabeth and Minnie returned home at about 5pm, and were asked where Fanny was, they said she had gone off with Baker. Mrs Adams and a neighbour, Mrs Gardener, went to look for her and met Baker near Flood Meadow. To the question 'What have you done with Fanny?' he replied 'Nothing'. Mrs Gardener wanted to report him to the police but Mrs Adams' suspicions were allayed by Baker's calm manner and air of respectability. At 7pm when Fanny had still not returned home a search was begun in the neighbourhood.

One of the searchers, a man named Gates, went into the hopfield near Flood Meadow. Finding a bloodstained dress he steeled himself to look farther, then to his horror found Fanny's head, and a little farther one of her legs, then her body, or what remained of it after all the organs had been cut out. These gruesome finds were taken to the Leather Bottle public house and then to the police station. The rest of the poor girl was found piece by piece the next morning.

According to the *Hampshire Chronicle* when Mrs Adams was told what had happened to Fanny she became 'nearly frantic', and ran to tell her husband, who was playing cricket, but collapsed on the way. When he heard the news Mr Adams rushed home, seized a loaded gun and went to the fields in search of Baker. Had he gone to Baker's office he would have found him there and the day probably would have ended with a second murder. As it was, when Mr Adams returned home the gun was taken from him by his neighbours who persuaded him to stay at home until the morning.

That evening, after speaking to Mrs Gardener and Minnie Warner and seeing the grisly evidence, Police Superintendent Cheney went immediately to Baker's office and to his surprise found him still there at 9pm. When told he was under suspicion Baker replied, 'I am innocent.' Cheney then arrested him, taking him out by the back door to avoid the large crowd that had gathered in the street. At the police station two small fancy knives were found in Baker's pockets; one with traces of blood. There were bloodstains on his shirt-cuffs and trousers for which Baker could offer no explanation. Further questioned about one of his socks and a trouser-leg being wet as if he had been standing in water he replied, 'Well, that won't hang me, will it?'

On the Sunday hundreds of people visited the meadows, hampering the local police in their search for clues and further parts of the child's body – there were not enough policemen in 1867 to keep sightseers away. The next day Baker was formally charged with murder. Superintendent Cheney then searched Baker's desk at his office and found his diary, in which the entry for Saturday read 'Killed a young girl. It was fine and hot.' Baker admitted the handwriting was his and said 'I did not mean to do so. I was intoxicated after I saw the women.' He probably meant that he had been to the Swan public house after meeting Mrs Gardener and Mrs Adams in the field. He had recently taken to drink and it was said that when intoxicated he showed signs of insanity.

The coroner's inquest was held on the Tuesday at the Duke's Head, Alton. Maurice Biddle, a clerk in Baker's office, said that at about 6pm on the Saturday Baker told him of his meeting with the women and said that it would be very awkward for him 'if the child was murdered'. This was an hour or more before the child's body was discovered and before there was any suggestion of murder. Later that evening Biddle told Baker that people in Alton were saying that he had killed Fanny Adams. Baker replied, 'Never, Maurice. It's a bad job for me, then.'

When the inquest jury returned a verdict of wilful murder Baker showed no sign of emotion. A large crowd surrounded the inn and two hours elapsed before it was thought safe to smuggle the prisoner out by the back door. Even then Baker and his police escort had to run at top speed to the police station, and the policemen were hit by several missiles.

On the Thursday Baker was examined in front of the local magistrates in Alton town hall and was committed for trial at the next Winchester assizes. He repeated that he was not guilty: 'I am as innocent as on the day I was born.' On leaving the town hall the police again had great difficulty in protecting Baker from a mob of Alton people who wanted to lynch him. It may not have been the first murder in Alton but it was certainly the first within living memory at that time.

When they reported the murder the national newspapers emphasized its barbarity and its apparent lack of motive. The *Standard* said it would rank in the records of crime with the murders by Burke and Hare, by Daniel Good and that of Maria Marten in the Red Barn. The *Morning Post* considered the crime the work of a lunatic, because a sane man could not have done it. The *Globe* thought that such a crime was a strong argument for capital punishment. The *Daily Telegraph* said that a more horrible crime had never been committed; it labelled the murderer a monster who should be 'put out of the way'. There is no doubt that the country was appalled by the story. All the newspapers were of the opinion that the murderer must have been insane. Indeed, had he been charged with the murder today Baker would probably have been found guilty, but insane.

In October further evidence was brought to the notice of the police. After the murder became known a little boy told his mother that at about 2pm on the day of the murder he had seen Baker leave the hop-garden and wash his hands in the stream. Seeing the boy watching him, Baker had told him to go away and repeated the order when the boy did not immediately obey. Baker then walked away in the direction of the turnpike road (where he was seen by the toll-keeper). But as presumably the boy did not see Baker again (unless he had been to the inquest) how did he identify him? For some unaccountable reason his mother told nobody of what the boy had seen until she let it out one day in a public house. On hearing the story the police searched the stream at the spot where the boy had seen Baker but found nothing. The boy's story revived interest in the murder, which by October had died down.

Professor Taylor of Guy's Hospital reported the results of

the examination of Baker's knives and clothes. He had found that the blood on them was human. As no other knife was found at the scene of the crime it was assumed that Baker had used one of his two small pocket-knives.

During his stay in Winchester prison awaiting trial Baker was said to be very talkative and uncomplaining. He frequently referred to the murder, saying his conscience was clear, and wondering who the murderer could be.

The trial was held on 5th December 1867 at Winchester Castle; Baker pleaded 'Not guilty'. The courtroom was full to overflowing and those who could not gain admission made so much noise that the judge threatened them with imprisonment. This had the desired effect and the trial proceeded peacefully. Most of the evidence was the same as at the inquest and before the magistrates in August. Baker's counsel made the best of a hopeless task by emphasizing the known insanity in Baker's family and the defects in Baker's own character. He said that Baker had once attempted suicide after a love affair, and his landlady gave evidence that he was always low in spirits and 'appeared wild'. Although the judge's summing-up took two hours, the jury was out for only 15 minutes. When the foreman announced the verdict of 'Guilty', Baker seemed unmoved and had nothing to say.

Baker's execution at Winchester gaol at 8am on Christmas Eve 1867, witnessed by more than 5,000 people, was one of the last to be held in public in England. (The last was on 26th May 1868 at Newgate, London.) The *Hampshire Chronicle* reported that a large proportion of the crowd were women, and that there were hundreds of working-class people from Winchester, Southampton and Portsmouth, a few shop-keepers and a small number of 'nondescripts'. The vast crowd watched in silence as the condemned man was led to the scaffold, the last prayer was said and the bolt withdrawn from under him.

In a letter to Fanny's parents, made public after his

execution, Baker expressed his deep sorrow and asked their forgiveness. He wrote that 'in an unguarded hour and not with malice aforethought, but being enraged with her crying' he killed Fanny 'without pain or struggle'. Mr and Mrs Adams said that they were willing to forgive Baker and expressed satisfaction with his confession.

Baker's decision to cut Fanny into pieces seems inexpli-

The gravestone for little Fanny Adams. Her brutal murder shocked the nation and was slow to fade from memory.

cable for his only hope of concealing the crime would have been to bury the body. It was suggested at the trial that he did so to hide the fact that he had violated her, but in his letter to her parents he denied the accusation. He had returned to his office in mid-afternoon for some reason (perhaps to get a knife), then paid a second visit to the fields, when he met Mrs Adams and Mrs Gardener. Did he cut up the body on this second visit? If not, what was the purpose of it?

The murder of Fanny Adams will always be remembered as one of the most horrible in the annals of crime, not only for its gruesomeness but also for its apparent lack of motive. To the very end Baker could not, or would not, say why he made such a savage attack on a small girl.

Soon after the murder, sailors in the Royal Navy were issued with tinned meat of an inferior quality. With the usual macabre humour of the lower deck they named this meat 'Sweet Fanny Adams'. The name stuck but over the years it acquired a different meaning, that of 'nothing' or 'worthless'. A sad memorial for a tragic tale.

Heaven or Hell

★

In 1880 large yellow posters appeared in Basingstoke. They read:

'O Yes! O Yes! O Yes!
To all you sinners who it may concern;
Two Hallelujah Lasses,
Being a Detachment of the Salvation Army,
Will open fire on Sin and Satan,
At the Factory, Brook Street, Basingstoke,
On Sunday, September 19th, 1880.'

The Salvation Army began as the Christian Mission, founded in 1865 by William Booth, a former Methodist preacher, with the aim of spreading the gospel to the poor people of the great cities of England by less conventional methods than those used by the established churches. At his headquarters in London's East End, Booth gathered around him a number of converts as willing helpers. In 1878 the name of the organization was changed to the Salvation Army.

The Army was subject to military rules and discipline and it was not immediately successful with its message of instant salvation. It never quite reached a working agreement with the Church of England, which founded the Church Army as a less belligerent organization. From its very inception the Salvation Army met with antagonism and intimidation, its members being cruelly ill-treated in many towns. Police and magistrates often turned a blind eye to this persecution but eventually the firmness of Sir William Harcourt, the Home

Secretary, brought a change of outlook on the part of the authorities.

In Basingstoke, opposition to the Salvation Army had been increasing for some time among certain sections of the community. Their noisy parades, held almost nightly, and their weekend gatherings antagonized some people but they had many sympathizers among liberal nonconformists. But no concerted effort to confront them was made until March 1881 when a pamphlet was circulated in the town entitled 'Declaration of War by the Massaganian Army against Dirty Dick's Army'. Supporters were requested to assemble in the market-place on the following Sunday at 10am. The opponents of the Salvation Army from now on called themselves 'Massaganians', believed to be an old Basingstoke word.

On the Saturday, all day, small groups of people loitered whispering on street corners and there was a strange air of expectancy in the town, but nothing occurred to which the police could take exception. On the Sunday (20th March) by 10am a huge crowd had assembled in the market-place waiting for the Salvationists to appear. As soon as they saw the Army turn the corner from Cross Street into New Street the crowd formed a procession behind a Union Jack and marched along Winchester Street to the top end of New Street. The two processions met in the middle of New Street with neither prepared to give way. The Union Jack disappeared in the mêlée and fighting broke out, during which one man had his arm broken.

The mayor, vicar and town councillors watched as the Salvationists forced their way into Winchester Street, but as the authorities took no action to stop the riot the Massaganian mob ignored them. On reaching the market-place the Army had to return along Church Street where the crush of people became intolerable. A plate-glass window was smashed and a man trampled on; although the police stopped many scuffles they made no arrests and their

38

presence was largely ignored. The mob pursued the Salvationists to their church, a disused silk mill in Brook Street known locally as the 'Factory'. The Army for their part seemed only too glad to reach the safety of the church and there they stayed for several hours.

At 2pm the Salvationists marched out of the church with an air of bravado, probably thinking that their opponents had dispersed, but they were sadly mistaken. Their Union Jack repaired, the Massaganians, many of them now drunk, marched down Church Street to meet them. The Salvationists and their sympathizers turned into Church Square and formed a ring for protection. This proved ineffective against the onslaught of the mob and soon fighting with fists and sticks broke out everywhere, with blood flowing freely. Hats were 'demolished in a most reckless manner' according to the *Hampshire Chronicle*.

So crowded was the square that it was not always clear who the opponents of the Salvationists really were; presumably mostly from the lower classes. One Salvationist, believing a respectable-looking gentleman to be a Massaganian, threw him to the ground and attempted to strangle him. The gentleman's friends and family rushed to his rescue and the riot now involved rich and poor, young and old. Despite calls by the mayor and the police superintendent for the fighting to stop, it continued for some time. The police again made no arrests, finding it hard in most cases to determine who was to blame, but contented themselves with trying to separate the two sides. Eventually the Massaganians marched away, giving three cheers for the mayor and singing a parody of a Salvationist hymn. The mob reassembled in the evening but this time the Army thought it best not to put in an appearance.

A meeting of Basingstoke's working men on the Monday passed a resolution calling for the Salvation Army to be protected by the law. When the Salvationists announced that come what may they would continue with their marches, 100 special constables were sworn in to prevent further trouble.

They were recruited from the town's leading tradesmen and the mayor made it clear that their duty was to protect the inhabitants and preserve the peace, rather than to protect the Salvation Army as the *Daily Telegraph* had suggested. The Salvationists announced their intention of marching again the following Sunday and excitement mounted in the town as the weekend approached.

On the Sunday at about 9.30am the special and the regular constables, some armed with staves, paraded in the square. A battery of the Royal Horse Artillery that happened to be stationed there added to the unusual spectacle. The special constables were ordered to the corner of Brook Street to meet the Salvationists who had just left the 'Factory'. Some of the constables formed up at the head of the Salvationists and the rest mingled with their procession, a tactical error that led to much recrimination. They marched up Church Street, followed by a crowd of Massaganians making as much noise as possible on fog-horns and tin whistles in an effort to drown the Salvationists' singing. From the market-place the Army marched down Wote Street and back to their church.

It was obvious long before this that the special constables were not being used to protect the inhabitants but to safeguard the passage of the Salvation Army, a task that they had been told they would not have to undertake. The special constables were by now angry and resentful because many of them were staunch Church of England members and yet here they were protecting a religious body they did not support or even approve of. When they had been dismissed they protested vigorously to the mayor.

Crowds of country people had flocked into Basingstoke by early afternoon and the Massaganians seemed to be more numerous, perhaps because they were making even more noise than ever. This time, when the Salvation Army emerged from the 'Factory' and marched to the corner of

Brook Street they saw to their alarm that two or three thousand people, accompanied by only a few special constables, were heading towards them. They retreated hastily to the 'Factory' and lined up facing it with their backs to a wall. Here they were hustled and jeered at by the crowd and things would have got out of hand had not the mayor read the Riot Act and called for the Royal Horse Artillery and the constables to clear the streets. This they did with some difficulty while the crowd, now in a good humour, laughed at their efforts. No damage or injuries were reported.

Further disorder was avoided by the banning of processions and assemblies in the town. On the following Sunday the Salvationists were prevented from marching by the local police. It was reported that the Salvationists stamped on the toes of the policemen to provoke them into taking action for a breach of the peace and so bring a test case to court, but the police perhaps wisely ignored them.

On Monday 11th April several cases of assault were brought before the Basingstoke magistrates. The first two cases involved two Salvationist supporters named Wallis, who according to several witnesses had without provocation attacked innocent bystanders. The mayor dismissed the first case and deferred judgement in the second, at which the prosecuting counsel said that he would take no further part in the cases still to be heard, implying that it would be a waste of time in front of this particular bench. (Two other members of the Wallis family happened to be local magistrates.)

Opposition to the Salvation Army came from members of other churches, from people who objected to the noise they made and most of all from publicans who would have been out of business if the Salvation Army had their way. The troubles at Basingstoke were surpassed in notoriety if not in violence by those at Whitchurch, which made national headlines for a time. No mercy was shown to the Army at Whitchurch; unlike at Basingstoke, the authorities were

THE
WAR ⚓ CRY
And Official Gazette of The Salvation Army.

[INTERNATIONAL HEADQUARTERS.] [Registered at the General Post Office as a Newspaper.] [101, QUEEN VICTORIA STREET, E.C.

No. 001. LONDON, SATURDAY, OCT. 26, 1889. PRICE ONE PENNY.

LIBERTY AT WHITCHURCH!

GIGANTIC AND UNPRECEDENTED DEMONSTRATION!   THOUSANDS OF SALVATIONISTS INVADE THE VILLAGE!!

Tremendous Meetings in the Square, before Melville Portal's Mansion, and in a Meadow!

Straight Talking from the Commandant and Field Commissioner.   Startling Torchlight Procession.

"Imagine a dockers' strike in Pompeii! Imagine the effect of suddenly turning a million magnifying microscopes on to a sample of innocent-looking London water! . . . . Think of Oklahoma, of Johnstown, of anything that gives the idea of sudden and mighty overwhelming of something very small, silent and sedate, and you will begin to be able to understand what Whitchurch was like when it was invaded by The Salvation Army."

It is thus that the London "Star," in a brilliant column report, from which we freely cull, hits off the overwhelming effect of our magnificent Liberty Demonstration in the now famous little Hampshire village.

"To Whitchurch!" was the battle cry which agitated the minds and quickened the pulse of every department of the London Headquarters, and resounded in many a corps.

The Chief Secretary had got "steam up" by Saturday morning, and as he danced along the passage through which the "Cry" representative was walking, advised the latter to take down

A Whole Legion of Pencils

to record the stirring scenes about to take place. As for the Field Secretary, was he not in his glory? Could business have been suspended,

Instead of only representatives from each, the various departments would have turned out wholesale; indeed, it would have been almost as easy to have got ten thousand as an invading force as the thousand or more who besieged Waterloo Station on Monday morning.

There was a rush for the twenty minutes past ten train, which was one of the most thoroughly Salvationist that ever graced the metals. Serg:

THE DEMONSTRATION AT LAVERSTOKE HOUSE, WHITCHURCH
(THE RESIDENCE OF MELVILLE PORTAL, ESQ.)

The determination and military style of the Salvation Army shown here in this illustration of a demonstration, taken from 'The War Cry', was perceived as belligerence and provoked a noisy and violent opposition.

determined to persecute and if possible suppress them.

In the Army's early days at Whitchurch its members were subjected to much harassment and ill-treatment. Their chief persecutors were the Irish labourers employed on the construction of the Newbury to Southampton railway. The landlord of The White Hart Hotel would get the labourers drunk and incite them to attack the Salvationists, who often finished up in the river. Superintendent Waters of the local police was also a fanatical opponent of the Salvation Army.

Things came to a head one day when the police broke up an Army meeting in the market place and arrested four members on a charge of obstruction. The local workhouse master gave evidence that he had to walk three yards out of his way to avoid them! The four were each fined twopence plus costs and when they refused to pay, were sent to prison for seven days. This set a useful precedent for Superintendent Waters and during the next five months 82 Salvationists were sent to prison.

On Monday 14th March 1889 about 2,000 Salvationists converged on Whitchurch, travelling there by excursion trains and by road. On arrival most of them formed a procession which marched to Laverstoke House to present a petition to Melville Portal, the chairman of the local magistrates. He was away at Winchester Quarter Sessions, and though the Army's solicitor went all the way to Winchester to deliver a letter to him, Portal refused to see him.

Meanwhile after holding a meeting at Laverstoke, the Salvationists and their supporters made their way back to Whitchurch. There they held another meeting addressed by Salvation Army leaders from London and passed a resolution calling for the same freedom accorded to the Salvation Army in the rest of the country. In the evening a large crowd assembled in a marquee for a 'liberty meeting' addressed by Commandant Herbert Booth. One of the speakers was the vicar of Whitchurch; he was obviously trying to sit on the fence, for he not only sympathized with the Salvation Army but also made excuses for the behaviour of the police and magistrates.

Eventually questions were asked in Parliament, by Gladstone and other Members. An appeal against the convictions was upheld by the Queen's Bench and costs were awarded against the Whitchurch magistrates. To celebrate this victory for common sense a rally was held at Whitchurch attended by 5,000 people. Twelve bands provided the music, which if they all played at the same time must have made the inhabitants of the town think hard about the outcome of the appeal.

The Great Blizzard

★

The British people have had to endure many severe winters, but only in recent times have sufficient records been kept to enable comparisons to be made. Only since the advent of newspapers can we be fairly sure of the accuracy of contemporary weather descriptions. There have been winters in modern times which have been disastrous because of the disruption to normal life, the misery that they inflicted and the loss of life that resulted from them, but few can equal that of 1881 for the chaos and dislocation that it caused.

In the first half of January 1881 the weather had been cold, with a thin covering of snow in many parts of the country, but pressure was rising to the east and falling to the west – an ominous sign in midwinter. On Monday the 17th the wind freshened later in the day and people in southern England looked apprehensively at the sky. Their fears were realised next day, for just before dawn a blizzard struck London and the south-east counties; driven by an east wind of sub-zero temperature and almost hurricane force it swept across the country. The snowflakes were not the usual soft variety but more like particles of ice, stinging the face and hands unmercifully as in a sandstorm. The snow was soon driven into deep drifts by the fierce wind.

Within a few hours, transport all over the country came to a standstill. Trams and other wheeled vehicles were unable to move and most railway lines soon became impassable. At 2.30 pm all main-line trains out of London were cancelled. The combination of frost, prolonged snow and a gale-force wind turned London and provincial towns into silent white

45

deserts in which there were few signs of life. Nobody ventured outdoors who had no business there; people watched from their windows as the wind piled the snow ever higher against the sides of their houses. The drifts eventually covered the windows so that lamps had to be lit; the fine snow penetrated every crack and crevice in the walls, piling up inside as well as out. The southern counties took the brunt of the blizzard, and in the gale more than 70 barges sank in the Thames in London. High tides flooded the districts on the south bank of the river, some houses being inundated to a depth of over five ft.

All activity in Southampton and Portsmouth soon came to a halt. On that Tuesday one and a half ft of snow fell in Southampton and the streets rapidly became deserted. People were blinded by the snow as they struggled along, scarcely able to stand upright in the gale; some were blown off their feet into snow-drifts. The wind tore branches from trees and blew down fences. Trams were suspended at midday, and horses and carts were quickly taken to shelter. Soon after leaving the George Inn the driver of the Romsey coach found that he could make no progress so he returned to the George and went to Romsey on the train. Schools were closed and those shops, offices and public houses that remained open had no customers. Dusk came unusually early but by then Southampton resembled a ghost town. The mail steamer *Alice,* which had set out for Le Havre, returned after an hour, its passengers having persuaded the captain to turn back. The railway line between Southampton and Portsmouth was blocked at Fareham.

The 11.20 am mid-Sussex train from Portsmouth became stuck in a snow-drift near Ports Creek. The driver uncoupled his engine from the carriages to try to force a way through the snow and then found that he was unable to reach them again. The 50 passengers on the train were trapped for several hours, with snow drifting as high as the carriage windows on one side. When the suffering travellers were finally released they struggled back to Portsmouth through waist-high snow. After 10 am on the Tuesday no train reached Portsmouth for the rest of that week; in the town the snowfall was said to be the heaviest since 1824. In the eastern suburbs householders found themselves completely snowed in and all business was suspended.

In Winchester old people declared that although they had known heavier snowfalls never had they experienced such unpleasant weather – the freezing wind completely numbed them. The train from London due at Winchester at 7pm on the Tuesday arrived four hours and 40 minutes late, after having been dug out of a drift near Micheldever, and trains continued to run three to four hours late that night. The next morning the 7am train from Woking reached Itchen Abbas before running into snow-drifts, finally arriving at

Portsmouth, deep in snow, in 1881.

Winchester six hours late with the daily newspapers, the belated delivery of which apparently upset some people more than anything else. Most of the main-line London to Southampton trains completed their journeys, unlike the London to Bristol trains, which got no further than Reading.

That Tuesday night the mail-cart left Alton for Winchester with two horses instead of the usual one and a vehicle with four wheels instead of two. In spite of these precautions the cart got stuck in a snow-drift on Morn Hill. The two drivers put the mail-bags on the horses' backs and delivered them safely to Winchester. On the return journey next day the men used only the horses. They took five hours from Alresford to Alton and arrived seven and a half hours late. Similar difficulties were experienced by the Stockbridge to Winchester mail, which arrived at 1.30 am, three and a half hours late, the driver having had to walk most of the way across fields. For the rest of the week the mails were running one day late, the roads being so blocked with snow that the carriers were unable to reach Winchester – in places the drifts were over ten ft deep.

The citizens of Winchester were trying to cope with several feet of drifting snow. The gale had blown it mostly to one side of the streets and blocked doorways, which were no sooner uncovered than blocked again. All roads out of Winchester were impassable; a baker and his delivery van came to grief on the Andover road, leaving all the loaves in the snow. The temperature that Tuesday night was 10°F – 22 degrees of frost.

A man going home to Twyford was halted by a ten ft high snow-drift and had to return to Winchester for the night. Twyford was cut off from the outside world by drifts five to ten ft deep, and although 50 men attempted to clear the Colden Common road it was not passable until the Friday. Alton was also cut off from all directions and some local postmen became lost in the drifts. At Andover the snowstorm lasted 36 hours and all the railway lines were blocked. The roads around Bishop's Waltham were snowbound to the tops of the hedges, and the only way to get from one village to another was across the fields. Some drifts were reported as being 15-16 ft deep. The only good news came from Romsey, where the snow was said to have caused no inconvenience because the mayor had ordered men to cart it away and throw it in the river.

One Salisbury to London train had a nightmare journey after passing through Andover. The railway cuttings became increasingly snowbound and somewhere beyond Whitchurch the engine had to be uncoupled to force a passage through the snow for 300 yards, then return for the carriages. This procedure was repeated all the way to Woking. Some of the passengers had foot-warmers; the driver remarked afterwards on the unconcern of the travellers, who rarely looked out of the windows at what was going on.

At Ryde on the Isle of Wight several vessels were blown from their moorings and two large colliers driven against the new pier. The railway line on the pier subsided for a distance of 140 yards and the damage amounted to £12,000. The colliers 'went to pieces', as did the luggage boat *Eclipse*. Bournemouth was hit severely by the blizzard, with drifts six ft deep. The Milford on Sea postman had a narrow escape from being frozen to death when he was found just in time. *The Times* with characteristic understatement described Tuesday's weather as 'exceedingly boisterous'.

The snow continued for a time on the Wednesday but the gale-force wind dropped considerably. A huge snow-clearing operation began in Southampton; thousands of cart-loads were emptied into the sea. The respite was only temporary for later on Thursday the snow returned in the second phase of the storm. The snowfall on the Tuesday had been one of the worst in living memory, but this was said to be even heavier. The wind was not so strong, however, so the snow was deposited more evenly. It fell for the rest of that day and night and streets that had just been cleared became blocked again. In Southampton the few trams that had restarted late on Wednesday and on Thursday morning were soon out of action. This second phase of the great blizzard affected only the south coast, but was just as severe as the first phase, another one and a half ft of level snow falling on the Thursday, a total of three ft in three days.

By Friday the drifts in Southampton averaged ten ft deep and the frost and snow halted all activity. There was much distress and hardship among the poor in the town. It was said that 8,000 people in the parish of St James alone required assistance, and soup kitchens were set up in Northam. The Inner Dock was frozen over for a week by 20 degrees of frost, and trams were out of action for several days. A meeting at Southampton was told by the mayor of the large number of outdoor workers now unemployed because of the bad weather, and that many of them had refused to clear the snow. The relieving officers were told to make a note of those workers when it came to making payments. A large number of the unemployed were nevertheless busy clearing the streets. Perhaps the only redeeming feature of the snowfall was that by Friday the town had a very picturesque appearance, and photographers were busy in High Street, the Dolphin Hotel being a popular target.

At Portsmouth six inches of snow fell in one hour early on Friday and many house roofs collapsed under the weight. It took 600 to 1,000 men with 100 carts to clear the estimated 650,000 tons of snow, and Prince Edward of Saxe-Weimar ordered troops from the garrison to help in clearing it. A train was eventually dug out after having been trapped between Gosport and Fareham for a week.

Many people made good use of the frost while it lasted. Skating took place on the Southampton Common reservoirs, and at Winnall near Winchester, where 2,000 people were either skating or watching, gangs of 'young roughs' pelted the skaters with snowballs. At Cowes on the Isle of Wight three days' newspapers arrived together on the Thursday; no shops were open in the town, and milk and fresh water were scarce. Most villages on the island were cut off for several days. Queen Victoria, staying at Osborne House, was definitely not amused when she found that she could not take her daily walk.

As a result of the blizzard more than 100 people died in southern England, several of them in Hampshire, from exposure and accidents, some of them frozen to death in snow-drifts. The average temperature on the Tuesday in southern England was 12°F – 20 degrees of frost. The storm lasted only two or three days, and the severe frost only a week, but for sheer unpleasantness the weather has probably never before or since been equalled.

Fire at The King's House

★

Towards the end of his reign King Charles II, tired of London, decided to live at Winchester whenever he could get away from his official duties. After all, as John Evelyn said, Winchester was 'infinitely preferable to Newmarket for prospects, air, pleasure, and provisions'. The King decided to build a palace on the site of Winchester castle, demolished soon after the Civil War. The mayor and corporation claimed the ownership of the site, which had been bought from Sir William Waller for £250. The real owner was probably Sir Henry Tichborne, who had made a prior claim to it.

In 1682 the corporation, realising what a great asset the palace would be to the city, sold the site to the King for the nominal sum of five shillings. In the King's opinion Sir Henry's claim was legitimate because he had defended the castle against Cromwell. Charles promised to pay him for the site, but died two years later and Sir Henry never received payment.

Charles invited Christopher Wren to design the palace, and the ground was cleared ready for building. On 23rd March 1683 as the King was as usual at the races, the mayor of Winchester laid the foundation stone. Charles and his brother James paid frequent visits in the next two years to see how the building was progressing. A magnificent avenue lined with mansions was projected, from the east front of the palace to the west front of the cathedral, and members of the nobility and gentry were induced to build houses in the city, some of which survive.

52

In plan and design the building was reminiscent of the Palace of Versailles, and Wren was obviously inspired by that masterpiece. The whole project, with its symmetrical design, was conceived in the grand manner of 17th century French palaces. There were to have been state apartments and council rooms, but the internal arrangements and positions of the staircases are uncertain because of the lack of authentic plans. Wren's original plans and drawings have been lost, and such as exist are unreliable evidence as to the intended layout of the buildings. The best engravings are on Godson's map of Winchester (1751) and in Milner's *The History and Survey of the Antiquities of Winchester*. The plan in Milner's book was drawn from an original elevation made by Wren himself, preserved at Brambridge House.

John Evelyn said that the palace was to have cost £35,000. There would have been a park and gardens on the west side – the land had been purchased for £7,180. Completed, the palace would have been at that time the most magnificent in the country ('the Versailles of England' wrote Milner).

When King Charles died 6th February 1685, the building of the palace was abandoned. Only the main building, forming three sides of a square, had been built, at a cost of £25,000. Although roofed it was incomplete, the domed vestibule and portico and the forecourt not started. James II and William III showed no interest in its completion; Queen Anne intended to complete it for her husband but he died before the work could begin.

John Evelyn saw the building in 1685: 'a stately fabric, of three sides and a corridor, all built of brick, and corniced . . . it has an incomparable prospect'. Daniel Defoe also saw it soon afterwards: 'the Building is begun, and the Front next the city carry'd up to the Roof, and cover'd; but the remainder is not begun'.

In the Seven Years War (1756-63) the building, now known as the King's House, was used as a prison for 5,000 prisoners at a time. During the American War of Independence

(1775-83) it housed 6,500 French and Spanish soldiers, and from 1792 to 1796 it was a home for 700 French priests, refugees from the Revolution, becoming a barracks in 1796. In 1809-11 it was reconstructed at a cost of £73,000 to hold 1,700 men, with an extra storey inserted in the state apartments. For almost 100 years the King's House served the needs of the Army, outwardly the same building but inwardly suffering the usual wear and tear associated with military occupation, until the night of Tuesday 18th December 1894.

A few minutes before midnight Private Jackson of the King's Royal Rifles returned to his barrack-room on the second floor behind the pay offices, passing through the cookhouse and up a flight of stairs to get to it. As he undressed quietly, so as not to wake his six room-mates, he thought he smelled burning but dismissed it as imagination. He fell asleep but after a few minutes woke up gasping and choking. The room was full of smoke and through a chink in the door he saw a flickering flame. He roused the others and wearing only a shirt ran down the unlit corridor to alert the sentry and buglers. The gas-lamps had been turned off as usual at 10.15 pm so the building was in darkness. As he blundered on, his foot caught in something and he fell and was overcome by the smoke; the next thing he knew was waking up in hospital.

The fire was soon located by the other men – the pay offices were ablaze. The first member of the fire brigade on the scene was fireman Polkinghorne, who lived not far away and had heard a policeman's whistle. Polkinghorne, the policeman and Captain Riley, the quartermaster, rushed into the barracks, meeting a messenger on his way to the police station to summon the fire brigade. Polkinghorne ran up to the pay offices and found one room full of smoke, with shelves and papers burning. He said afterwards that if there had been a good supply of water he could have doused the fire there and then. But no water was available, not even a bucketful, and he could do nothing until the fire brigade arrived.

Those who first saw the fire from outside the building also thought it was quite small. A policeman in St James's Lane said 'You could have put it all in a bucket.' But they were deceived by the angle at which they saw it, for there is no doubt that when Jackson and his mates became aware of the fire, one pay office was well and truly ablaze. The layout of the building favoured the spread of the fire, as did the weather that night. A strong wind was blowing, with squally showers, entering the building through vents and cracks and blowing down the long draughty corridors. The nearest sentries to this south wing were those at Castle Hill and the Southgate Street gates.

The buglers sounded the call 'Fire' to alert the men responsible for handling the fire-engines, and then the call 'Assemble' to gather the rest of the men on the parade-ground. Most of the 600-700 men arrived half-dressed – some without tunics, some without overcoats, some without trousers, some with socks but no boots. They stood in the cold and wet while the officers concerned themselves with the fire. The men who fetched the two fire-engines wheeled them to the fire hydrant and attached the hoses in record time – but there was no water. They watched in frustration as the fire spread, fanned by the strong wind.

When the messenger reached the police station at the Guildhall in High Street at 12.16 am Police Sergeant Jelliff summoned the volunteer fire brigade by means of electric bells, and they arrived within a few minutes. (The fire station was also at the Guildhall.) Jelliff meanwhile hurried to the stables for horses and sent for a party of soldiers to haul the steam fire-engine to the barracks in case there was delay with the horses. This sounds a long-winded business compared with today, but it took only a few minutes.

On arriving at the barracks the brigade connected the steam fire-engine to the main water-tank in the inner square

The King's House, Winchester, the building planned as the 'Versailles of England', seen here after the fire of 1894.

of the central block, but because of the dense smoke driven by the wind they had to retreat to avoid being suffocated. Watched by the Water Company officials they then connected the engine to the hydrant in the square, but as the military brigade had already discovered there was very little water from that source. By now the fire extended the whole width of the south wing, and within 20 minutes of the fire brigade being called the roof was ablaze from end to end. The fire was now completely out of control and no amount of water could have saved the building. An attempt to quell the flames by running a hose up the stairs to the pay offices had failed through lack of water. Water from the first hydrant, which came from the St James's Lane main, had proved quite inadequate but when the hydrants supplied from the Romsey Road and Castle Hill mains were tried there was a good supply.

As the fire rapidly spread and worked its way towards the roof the men tried to rescue belongings, valuables and pets from their barrack-rooms. Orders were given to save objects on the ground floor, which was not yet on fire, but some men managed to get upstairs. It was a risky and dangerous task, for not only was it dark (apart from the light from the flames) but also it was full of smoke. One man rescued a litter of puppies and their mother. The Rifle Corps sergeants retrieved all their valuable cups and trophies but not their brand-new billiard table. The Hampshire Regiment sergeants were not so lucky – they lost everything. The whole of the barracks library went up in flames – about 3,000 volumes. Everything in the canteens was lost except the canteen stewards' books, and most of the band instruments were destroyed. The hardest work was the removal of the contents of the armoury and the quartermaster's stores into the barrack hospital. The officers and men were involved in a race against time, with the fire spreading rapidly and filling the whole building with dense smoke.

The fire brigade captain wrote in his report afterwards that 'it is doubtful had we any amount of water whether we should have been able to stay the progress of the flames', and the farcical procedures with the hydrants certainly put paid to any hope of saving the building. Having reached the roof the blaze spread rapidly, unchecked by dividing walls. Above the roar of the flames and the crash of falling tiles and bricks the clock over the main entrance was heard to strike the hour. Shortly after 1 am the roof fell in, carrying with it the cupola above the clock, which stopped at that moment. Floor by floor the fire descended and spread sideways so that by 3 am the entire block was enveloped in a mass of flames. Afer the fire it was found that the upper walls were made of rubble encased in brick, unlike the lower walls, which were of solid brick.

Many local residents gathered at St James's Terrace where they watched the fire for hours. From St Giles's Hill it was an unforgettable sight, looking rather like a distant Black

Country furnace. At St Cross, people could read outdoors by the light of the fire and at Eastleigh windows were illuminated by it.

Those in the barrack square watched with sadness and horror as the whole interior of the building was consumed by the flames and parts of the roof came crashing down, accompanied by the frequent explosion of cartridges. At one point the sergeants' cherished billiard table fell to the ground floor with a crash. Sparks, burning ashes and paper were blown by the strong wind in a constant stream across the city, even as far as Easton and Winnall. So thick were these in High Street that residents had to keep a watch on their houses, but the frequent heavy showers of rain may well have prevented any other fires.

There were fears that the fire would reach the magazine in a separate ground-floor building near the quadrangle, but fortunately it was prevented from doing so. At the height of the blaze a cat was seen to jump from a top-storey window to the ground and walk away seemingly unhurt. Next morning another cat was seen alive and well, high up in the ruined building, and was rescued with some difficulty.

When the fire brigade realised the futility of trying to save any of the main building they turned their attention to the nearby County buildings, which stood in some danger. The walls of the Great Hall, which at its nearest point was only 14 ft from the burning building, were said to be too hot to touch. The portraits in the magistrates' room were removed for safety and men stood by ready to take down the ancient Round Table. At 5 am the flames at the east end of the north wing were dangerously close, but strenuous efforts by the fire brigade kept them at bay. The brigade finally gave up at 11 am, there being no further danger, but the walls and debris smouldered for the next two days.

On the Thursday morning visitors found that the building had been gutted. A gap 14 ft wide extended from top to bottom of the south wing at the spot where the fire had started. An angle of the building had fallen, exposing gas-pipes, charred beams and staircases that clung to sagging supports. The outer walls looked very insecure and the frequent sound of falling masonry kept visitors at a respectful distance. In the courtyard the cooks were preparing an alfresco meal for the weary and smoke-blackened men, and two stalls were selling apples and ginger beer.

The cause of the fire was thought to be a faulty flue running through the pay offices. It was established that all fires in the offices had been put out when the clerks left the previous evening and that no blame attached to any of the staff. At the inquiry it transpired that there were no buckets of water in the passages and corridors. The damage was estimated at £100,000. By amazing good fortune there were no deaths or serious injuries, the worst being a sprained ankle suffered by an officer. The *Hampshire Chronicle* described the fire as 'the most terrible calamity and unparalleled catastrophe in Winchester's modern history'.

The Water Company blamed the shortage of water on those in charge at the barracks. It seems that it was the practice to shut off the water at the mains at 4 pm every day, causing the tanks and service pipes to empty. When the water at the mains was turned on again the tanks and pipes had to refill before there was a head of water at the hydrants. The other cause of the shortage was that the bypass valve at the Romsey Road main was not used, so that when the water at the main was turned on it passed through the meter instead of straight through to the barracks. The Company said that nevertheless if the water at the main had been turned on right from the start there would have been sufficient even going through the meter. A key for turning on the bypass valve was kept in a glass case at the Romsey Road entrance; somebody had smashed the glass and tried without success to use the key, which was never found. For a small sum of money the system could have been altered so that the hydrants filled up before the tanks and pipes, but as always those in charge were wise after the event.

The military authorities on the other hand asserted that the man deputed to open the bypass valves in Romsey Road and St James's Lane did so speedily, so who was right? A messenger sent to the waterworks asked for full pressure to be applied and for the water to the city mains to be cut off, but nearly an hour passed before the water was at full pressure. It seems that the barracks waterman also made an error by opening the two-inch-diameter bypass valve at St James's Lane instead of the three-inch valve at Romsey Road.

So a blaze that a few buckets of water could have doused, resulted in the worst fire in the city's history. As always with man-made disasters, the root cause was someone's incompetence or lack of foresight.

Happily though, not all was lost, for the new barracks, rebuilt in 1899-1902, incorporated some of the columns, architrave and frieze from the old building.

The Saviour of
Winchester Cathedral

★

In the late autumn of 1905 rumours and speculations about the deteriorating condition of Winchester Cathedral appeared in many newspapers. On 8th November a letter from William Furneaux, the Dean of Winchester, was printed in *The Times* and other national newspapers; it was the first official confirmation that something was seriously wrong with the building. In his letter the Dean appealed for funds to help with the cost of repairs, which he estimated at £20,000. The letter was accompanied by photographs of the timber beams already shoring up the east end of the cathedral, and the newspaper headlines speculated that the building might be in danger of collapse.

The same letter was printed in the *Hampshire Chronicle* that week, followed by a long and detailed account of a structural investigation and the remedies proposed to counter the threatened subsidence and collapse of the east end of the cathedral. Of the £20,000 estimated cost £3,000 had already been promised, but £20,000 was to prove only a small fraction of the final cost of repairs.

The Dean said that the south wall of the retrochoir (the area behind the choir) was in a dangerous state because of subsidence of the east end, caused partly by insufficient buttressing in its original construction and partly by the insubstantial foundations on which the building had been erected. The walls rested on a bed of marly clay and peat ten ft below ground level, permanently waterlogged. Thomas Jackson, the Diocesan Architect, had recommended that the walls should be secured by bonding and grouting, then underpinned to a bed of gravel 16 ft below ground.

The Dean pointed out that although some of the cracks in the walls had been known for hundreds of years, new cracks had appeared and plaster had fallen in the crypt and the south transept. It was now time to face the problem before it got worse. He speculated whether the improvement in the city's drainage system had lowered the water table and hastened the subsidence.

Francis Fox, the consulting engineer, was the man who conceived the idea of using a diver to underpin the foundations with concrete laid directly on the gravel. Fox was an expert on foundations, particularly those under water, and had worked on the Mersey Tunnel. He recruited two divers, Walker and Rayfield, from the firm of Siebe, Gorman & Co., the diving specialists.

Fears had been expressed by the Dean that the use of a pump to remove water from under the walls was causing more damage; Jackson did not think so. After an inspection by Fox, however, it was decided to use a diver to remove the bottom layer of peat and to place the bags of concrete on the gravel. This would speed up the work and obviate any possible further damage by pumping. The diver started work on 6th April 1906 and in May the *Sphere* printed the first photograph of him at work.

The *Hampshire Chronicle* of 7th April, reporting that the diver was working to underpin the foundations, explained that after removing the peat bed he would put down four layers of concrete bags; when the water was then pumped out, concrete blocks and bricks would be built up to the footings of the walls. It also reported that £14,000 had been received as a result of the appeal for money.

The Times of 12th April printed a letter from the Dean together with a long report by Thomas Jackson. The Dean was at pains to scotch the rumours and exaggerations appearing in the newspapers, and attempted to alleviate the anxiety felt by many people as to the state of the cathedral. He also revised his estimate of the final cost to £30,000, little knowing that the final cost in 1912 would amount to £113,000 – £4.2 million in present-day values. (Compare that with the recent appeal for £7 million.)

In his report Jackson explained that most of the trouble had been caused by the original foundations laid down by the Norman builders. They consisted of 'two layers of trees laid across one another in a mass of loose chalk – many are soft and decayed but others are still sound.' Had this timber layer been wider than the walls all might have been well, but it had been crushed into the soft ground above the peat, causing the now all too apparent settlement of the east end of the building. The underlying gravel bed slopes down towards the east, so that whereas the west end of the cathedral rested directly on it, at the east end there was a layer of peat five ft thick above the gravel. At the east end of the cathedral the gravel bed was 29 ft below the floor of the retrochoir (21 ft below ground level and 14 ft below the water level). The cathedral had therefore slipped eastwards, causing great cracks in the walls.

The report explained that when the peat layer was pierced the water underneath was forced up through it to a level corresponding to the local water table. The trouble with using a powerful pump to remove the water was that it also brought out sand and soil, thus endangering the footings of the walls, hence the decision that the diver should remove the bottom two feet of the peat layer and cover the gravel bed with concrete bags. The workmen would then pump out the water and place concrete blocks and bricks on top of the bags.

The chief diver in this operation was William Walker, whose statue stands in the retrochoir of the cathedral. There are many statues in England, to persons deserving and un-deserving, but if anyone ever merited one it was William Walker. It is sufficient to say that single-handed he underpinned almost the whole of the east end of the cathedral and saved it from eventual collapse. He worked from 6th April 1906 to 8th September 1911, each working day consisting of two four-hour shifts, during which he spent two periods of three hours under water.

Walker was born in 1864 and at the age of 23 began his diving career at Portsmouth dockyard. He joined Siebe, Gorman & Co. in 1892 and became one of their best divers, without much doubt one of the most experienced divers in England. He was very conscientious, a fact verified by Francis Fox whenever he went down to inspect the diver's work. Walker must have been very fit and strong – all the more tragic that he died of influenza in the great epidemic of 1918.

Walker worked in complete darkness for most of the time. When he started work in the morning the water was clear and he could see what he was doing but it soon became clouded by sediment. The drifts or trenches that he worked in were only three to four ft wide but up to 20 ft long; often he had to work lying down and always in a cramped position. The weight of his diving suit and equipment amounted to 200 pounds but that was partly offset by the buoyancy of the water; an experienced diver like Walker could control his buoyancy by allowing air to enter the space in the middle of his diving-suit. He was connected to his assistant above by an air-line and a 'breast-rope' for signalling. Walker became very proficient at excavating the peat layer, levelling the gravel bed and laying the bags of cement concrete, all in pitch-darkness. The bags were slit open so that water would be absorbed by the concrete, which when it had set after 24 hours sealed off the inflow of water. The water in the drift was then pumped out and the blocks of concrete and the bricks laid down.

William Walker became well known not only locally but also further afield, through newspaper reports and articles. This in turn attracted many visitors to the cathedral to see

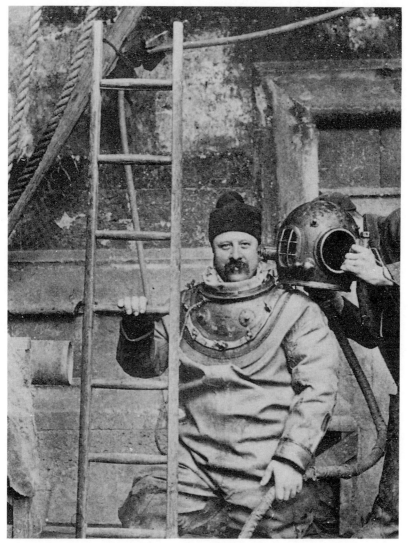

William Walker, the pioneering diver who laboured for five years to save Winchester Cathedral from the threat of collapse.

what was going on and perhaps to catch a glimpse of the diver. The publicity also helped to swell the appeal fund, which reached £25,000 by December 1906. But as fast as the money came in so did the estimate of the cost increase, and it now stood at £50,000.

The newspapers, although they sometimes exaggerated their reports, were not always wrong in their facts and forecasts. In 1907 they reported that the whole of the north transept would have to be underpinned. Jackson immediately denied this and hurried to Winchester to investigate. A few weeks later he recommended that very same course of action, describing how the foundations of the transept had given way causing the side walls to lean outwards. It was then found that the south transept required the same treatment; this meant that the estimate of the total cost would have to be revised to £85,000. But the appeal fund still stood at £25,000. The Ecclesiastical Commissioners had donated £5,000 and King Edward VII £250. Because of the lack of money some of the workers had to be dispensed with in October 1907; about 60 masons and labourers were laid off but William Walker continued with his work. In June 1908 the Winchester National Pageant, held in the grounds of Wolvesey Castle, raised £2,500 for the appeal fund.

In September 1909 *The Times* once again printed a letter from Dean Furneaux appealing for more money. He pointed out that although £76,000 had already been subscribed another £23,000 was still needed, otherwise the underpinning would have to come to a halt. This money would also cover the cost of erecting buttresses against the south wall of the cathedral; they had not been thought necessary when the cathedral was originally built. When it was all finished in 1912 people wondered where the money had gone as there was little to show for it, except for the buttresses and some new vaulting in the nave. It had of course been spent mostly on the underground work – the concrete bags, concrete blocks and bricks, and the wages of the divers and workmen.

Walker's final task was the underpinning of the new buttresses along the south wall; he finished the last one on Friday 8th September 1911 and left Winchester the next day, a rather more famous man than when he had arrived five and a half years previously. He told a local reporter: 'I haven't much of a story to tell.' The following year he returned for the thanksgiving service. He had completed a task unique in the history of British engineering, laying about 25,800 bags of concrete (an average of 90 a week), on which the workmen deposited about 115,000 concrete blocks and 900,000 bricks.

On 15th July 1093 Winchester cathedral had been consecrated. On 15th July 1912 a service of thanksgiving was held to celebrate the recent preservation work that had saved the building from impending disaster. The service, attended by King George V and Queen Mary, made headline news in all the national newspapers. The *Daily Express* headlines were: 'MAN WHO SAVED A CATHEDRAL', 'THE KING'S TALK WITH A DIVER', and 'YEARS IN THE DARK'.

The King and Queen came by train to Winchester, then drove in an open carriage down High Street to the Guildhall, where the Recorder of Winchester read an address in front of a guard of honour formed by the King's Royal Rifles. The King spoke to a few veterans who had taken part in the Crimean War and the Indian Mutiny nearly 60 years before.

The royal party then proceeded to the cathedral for the service. The sermon was given by the Archbishop of Canterbury and in it he singled out for special mention the names of Herbert Ryle, Bishop of Winchester, Dean Furneaux, Thomas Jackson, Francis Fox and William Walker. After the cathedral service the King spoke to all those who were involved in the preservation work, including William Walker, who said afterwards that it was the proudest moment of his life and that he felt the work had been well worth doing.

The Schneider Trophy

★

Flying Officer Waghorn began to congratulate himself. His Supermarine S6 seaplane was behaving perfectly, its engine temperature steady at 95° centigrade and its speed well over 300 mph with the throttle some way below maximum. One lap to go he thought, as he passed the start and finish line at Ryde pier, and he would probably win the Schneider Trophy for Great Britain. He turned at the Seaview pylon and aimed for the pylon south of Hayling Island; as he did so the engine cut out but picked up immediately. As he approached the pylon the engine started to miss. It could mean only one thing – he was running out of petrol. He pulled back the joystick to gain height, rounded the pylon and headed for the Southsea pylon, with the engine spluttering on half-throttle.

Rounding the Cowes pylon the engine stopped altogether and Waghorn landed the aircraft on the water. He sat in the cockpit in bewilderment and despair. The engineers must have miscalculated the amount of fuel required for he had carried out his instructions not to use full throttle to conserve fuel, but who would believe him? He would be blamed for this calamity. Now it was all up to Flying Officer Atcherley to record the best average lap time in the other Supermarine S6.

This was Saturday 7th September 1929 and Great Britain and Italy were engaged in an exciting race for air supremacy – the prize was the Schneider Trophy. The course was a quadrilateral measuring 50 kilometres over the Solent marked by buoys in the water and four pylons on ships. Seven laps had to be flown by each contestant and the one achieving the best average speed of all his seven laps would win the Trophy for his country.

Both Great Britain and Italy had entered their full quota of three aircraft: Waghorn and Atcherley in Supermarine S6s and Flight Lieutenant D'Arcy Grèig in a Supermarine S5; Lieutenants Cadringher and Monti and Warrant Officer Dal Molin in three Macchi seaplanes – two M67s and an M52R. Waghorn, Atcherley and Greig were fellow instructors at the Central Flying School and famous for their aerobatics at air displays.

It all began in 1913 when the first Schneider Trophy contest, held at Monaco, was won by a French Deperdussin. The Trophy had been presented by Jacques Schneider, son of an armaments manufacturer, who became an aviation enthusiast and dreamed of a future dominated by seaplanes. Ironically he died in 1928 in poverty and obscurity at the time when vast sums of money were being spent by the competing nations to secure the Trophy.

Five countries competed in the Trophy's 18 year history but never all in the same year. The winners had been France in 1913, Great Britain in 1914, Italy in 1920 and 1921, Great Britain in 1922, USA in 1923 and 1925, Italy in 1926 and Great Britain in 1927. The rules stipulated that a country winning three times in five successive contests could keep the Trophy, so Great Britain was keen to win in 1929 and follow it up with another win in 1931. At Venice in 1927 the race had been won by Flight Lieutenant Webster in a Supermarine S5 at an average speed of 282 mph.

Today Waghorn had been the first away; the others would follow at 15 minute intervals, each country alternately. Second away was Dal Molin in the M52R – Waghorn on his third lap had seen him cross the starting-line and had followed him round the course, overtaking him on the Cowes-Ryde straight on the very next lap. Now, as he sat in his cockpit, Waghorn wondered whether D'Arcy Greig in the S5 could outpace Dal Molin, not knowing that Greig on his first lap, flying flat out, was slower than Dal Molin.

When the launch came to pick him up the crew were waving and shouting excitedly. What were they so happy about? Had Greig pulled it off? Then he heard the truth – he had run out of fuel while flying an extra, unnecessary lap. He had miscounted and the engineers in fact had calculated correctly the amount of fuel required. Furthermore his average speed for the seven laps was 328.63 mph, which could easily prove a winning speed. In 1927 Webster had made exactly the same mistake but he completed an extra lap without running out of fuel.

Neither Dal Molin nor Greig knew what had happened to Waghorn so they both tore round the circuit at full throttle. In the end Dal Molin was the faster by 2 mph (284 and 282 mph respectively), but both were well below Waghorn's speed. Cadringher in the first Macchi M67 was next away but soon began to suffer from the effects of his exhaust fumes, which on this left-handed circuit blew back into the cockpit at every turn, half-blinding and suffocating him, so that he had to retire on his second lap.

Flying Officer Atcherley was next in the second S6; despite a poor first lap through losing his goggles he achieved an average speed over the seven laps of 325.54 mph, but was disqualified for cutting inside the Seaview pylon on his first lap. The last of the six competitors, Lieutenant Monti, was forced to retire on his second lap by a broken water-joint which scalded him with boiling water. So Waghorn won comfortably and there were great celebrations in the British camp.

The winning aircraft, the Supermarine S6, was developed from the S4, which gained the world air-speed record for seaplanes in 1925, and from the S5, which won the 1927 Schneider contest and also set up speed records. It was built by Supermarine Aviation at Southampton and designed by R J Mitchell, destined for even greater fame and success as the designer of the Spitfire fighter, first flown in 1936. The

S6 was powered by a 1900 hp Rolls-Royce engine and the S5 by an 875 hp Napier Lion engine. The S6 was larger than the S5 and nearly twice as heavy when loaded; its fuel tanks were in the floats. The first of the S6 aircraft was launched on 5th August, only a month before the race, and in the first flight tests the pilot had been unable to get the aircraft off the water.

The night before the race a cylinder-block had to be changed on one of the S6s, an all-night task undertaken by the Rolls-Royce mechanics who luckily had arrived from Derby in time. Another defect, water leaking from the wing radiators, was treated by pouring Johnson's patent 'Neverleak' into them. There were to have been two other aircraft available for the British team, two Gloster VI seaplanes, but they had to be withdrawn the night before the race because of persistent troubles with both fuel systems. They had been specially built for the race and were tested for the first time on 25th August. The race was preceded by navigability trials in which all the aircraft underwent a series of severe tests on the water and in the air, and then remained moored for six hours to test their seaworthiness. After the tests no further modifications of any kind were allowed.

The race itself was conducted efficiently and with precision, but for the hundreds of thousands of people who flocked into Hampshire on the Friday and Saturday arrangements were chaotic. Throughout Friday, Friday night and Saturday morning the coast of the Solent was invaded by people arriving by train, car, bicycle and on foot. Traffic on the roads was nose to tail, and that was in the days when the number of vehicles in the country was only one-tenth of the total today. Cars from the West Country were advised to head for Lee-on-the-Solent and Gosport, from the north for Southsea and from the east for Hayling Island. This advice was not strictly followed, resulting in congestion at crossroads, but no serious traffic jams were reported.

Southsea afforded the best vantage point and people poured in on the Friday and Saturday. It acquired the nickname 'Elastic town' when it seemed able to accommodate an infinite number of visitors. When all its hotel and guest-house bedrooms had been booked visitors paid to sleep in bathrooms, kitchens and caravans. The Council arranged for schools and drill-halls to be made available for those without beds. Men with binoculars were going from house to house offering five shillings in exchange for a perch on the owner's chimney-pot during the race.

The best viewpoint of all was the beach. The four mile-long stretch of sands was expected to hold half a million spectators – perhaps nobody had thought about the incoming tide. South Parade pier could accommodate 5,000 people. The Council was expecting 20,000 cars – 3,000 of them could be parked on Southsea Common. Temporary grandstands were erected wherever there was room and seats in them cost five shillings. From Waterloo and Victoria 250 special excursion trains left for Southampton and Portsmouth. The race was watched by the Prince of Wales and the Prime Minister, Ramsay MacDonald. Afterwards the Prime Minister said: 'We are going to do our best to win again.' Among the many congratulations to pilots, engineers and constructors nobody paid tribute to Johnson's 'Neverleak'!

Preparations for the 1931 contest were beset by financial and political difficulties. At first the British Government wanted nothing to do with it, refusing financial backing, the loan of aircraft and the use of RAF pilots. Even when the French and Italian Governments declared their intention of competing the British Government refused to budge, despite pleas from British aircraft constructors and the Royal Aero Club. It was only after Lady Houston, the widow of a millionaire shipowner, offered to finance the British entry that the Government belatedly agreed to give the race its blessing.

The Supermarine S6 (N248) seen here on a beaching trolley at Calshot.

Great Britain now had only seven months to prepare for the race, which would again be held over the Solent. Two new aircraft, designated S6B, were ordered from Supermarine, their design based on the S6 of 1929, and two of the old S6s were to be modified as S6As. After many trials and modifications all the machines were ready a few days before the race. Meanwhile the French and Italian Governments sought to postpone the race because their aircraft would not be ready in time. The Royal Aero Club refused their request and a week before the race the French and Italian entries were withdrawn. This meant that a British aircraft had only to fly round the course successfully to retain the Trophy.

It was decided that one of the British aircraft would also make an attempt on the world air-speed record. Flight Lieutenant Boothman was selected for the Trophy flight in an S6B and Flight Lieutenant Stainforth for the record attempt in the other S6B. If Boothman broke the Schneider speed record there were no plans for another run by one of the other aircraft; only if he failed would an S6A fly round the course to make sure of the Trophy and then the second S6B would make an attempt on the world record.

On Saturday 12th September the Hampshire coast was packed with spectators even though the race was now simply a fly-over. The flights were postponed, however, because of choppy water and rain and the spectators went home disappointed. Most of them returned on the Sunday, when the weather was calm and dry. Boothman completed his seven laps without incident at an average speed of 340 mph, although he was not sure whether he had completed the full quota of laps – the third year in succession that the winning pilot had similar doubts. Stainforth then made his successful attempt on the world speed record, achieving 379 mph. A fortnight later with a new engine and special fuel he set a new record of 407.5 mph.

Commemorative flights are held over the Solent every year or so but they cannot recapture the enormous excitement and interest aroused by those original contests.

The Southampton Garage Murder

★

On Thursday 10th January 1929 Henry Passmore walked down Grove Street, Southampton, in a fairly contented frame of mind. He had just been appointed the local representative of the Wolf's Head Oil Company, and was on his way to the garage at No 42 where his predecessor, Vivian Messiter, had kept his motor car and stock of lubricating oil. Passmore wondered idly what had become of Messiter, who had not been seen or heard of since 30th October the previous year. Perhaps he had left the country; he was known to have travelled abroad in the past and it was said that he had a wife who lived in the United States.

Passmore found the garage padlocked but with the help of a neighbour forced it open. Inside he found Messiter's car, a large number of oil drums and – a dead man, lying on his back, his face eaten away by rats and unrecognizable. Horrified, Passmore hurried out to call the police. Returning to the garage, he discovered that the car's ignition was on and that the petrol tank was empty, as if the engine had been left running perhaps to ensure death by carbon monoxide poisoning, although this was never proved.

The body was identified at the mortuary as Messiter. Albert Parrott, with whom he lodged, recognised his clothes, his shoes and the colour of his hair. Parrott had reported Messiter missing to the police on 1st November, and a week later, at the request of Messiter's head office, he and two police officers went to Grove Street to find out whether the motor car was still there. The garage was locked but they could see the car through a window. Assuming that Messiter had gone away on business the police left, and did nothing more about the missing man.

Messiter was by all accounts a quiet, respectable man of regular habits who had been a captain in the Canadian Army in the First World War. A strange fact came to light during subsequent investigations into his character – Southampton Chamber of Commerce had elected him as a member while he was lying dead in the garage.

The Southampton police were confronted with a murder mystery, for undoubtedly Messiter had been killed by a person or persons unknown, it was thought initially by a shot in the head. As ten precious weeks had been lost, Scotland Yard was called in, and Chief Inspector Prothero was sent to investigate. *The Times*, whose headlines on the Saturday were 'MAN SHOT IN A GARAGE: SUSPECTED MURDER AT SOUTHAMPTON', reported that a post-mortem examination had revealed a bullet wound in the head. On the following Monday *The Times* again referred to a shot in the head, the theory then held by the police.

Even after a hammer was found in the garage the police still thought in terms of a bullet wound. The *Hampshire Chronicle* said that it was fairly certain Messiter had been shot from behind, and stressed the importance of finding the bullet. Because it was still missing after a long search, the *Chronicle* suggested that the murderer may have taken it away. The matter was resolved when the hammer was examined by Sir Bernard Spilsbury, the famous pathologist, who said that Messiter probably had been struck down with it while in a stooping position. Following this statement the *Hampshire Chronicle* said that the use of a hammer suggested that the crime was unpremeditated, otherwise a more suitable weapon would have been used. (If this *was* the murder weapon it had proved remarkably effective.) A photograph of the hammer, an engineer's riveting hammer of Continental type, appeared in the newspaper with a request from the police for anyone who could identify it to come forward.

On the seat of the car were an exercise book and an invoice book with carbon sheets at the back on which were names and addresses and orders for oil. These were at first thought to be the names of Messiter's customers, but further enquiries revealed that the names and addresses were all fictitious. Several pages had been torn out of both books. One page in the exercise book had indentations made by a pencil or pen on the preceding page, which had been torn out. These indentations were deciphered as the words: 'October 28, 1928. Received from the Wolf's Head Oil Co. commission on Cromer and Bartlett 5 galls. at 6d. 2/6. W.F.T.' But who was W.F.T.?

The mystery was solved by a letter, found among Messiter's private papers in his rooms, dated 23rd October 1928. It was headed 'W.F. Thomas, 5 Cranbury Avenue, Southampton' and read: 'Sir, Re your advt. of the present inst. Being in the Motor Trade, and having a good connection amongst farmers and garage proprietors, I am sure I can do you good service in the oil lines. I am constantly asked my opinions of such, and I am sure I can build up a good connection.' W.F.T. was undoubtedly W.F. Thomas. The advertisement was traced to the *Southern Daily Echo:* 'Wanted, experienced MAN, with knowledge of local conditions, to sell lubricating oils, on commission.'

Further evidence came to light when a tiny screwed-up piece of paper was found on the garage floor. On it were the words 'Mr. W.F. Thomas. I shall be at Grove Street at 10am, but not at noon. V. Messiter.' All clues now pointed to the mysterious W.F. Thomas. The police called at 5 Cranbury Avenue, a guest-house kept by a Mrs Horne, who said that a couple named Thomas had stayed with her from 20th October to 3rd November the previous year. The forwarding address they had given proved to be fictitious. From her description the police were able to issue particulars of

Thomas, and almost immediately were rewarded by a message from a firm of contractors at Downton near Salisbury, Charles Mitchell and Sons, who had employed Thomas as a motor mechanic for several weeks from October to December 1928. He had left suddenly, in suspicious circumstances, the day after the wages for Mitchell's employees had disappeared.

The police then found another clue in Thomas's lodgings – a sheet of paper with the name 'Podmore' written on it and another with an address in Manchester. An enquiry at that address revealed that Podmore had been employed there until 17th October 1928. The police now felt sure that 'Thomas' was Podmore, whom they knew from his past record of petty crime.

A week after the discovery of the body the police traced Podmore to a hotel in London through his girl friend Lily Hambledon (alias 'Mrs Thomas') at Stoke-on-Trent, who told them where to find him. Podmore assured the police that he was in fact on his way to Southampton to tell them what he knew of Messiter. He admitted having been at Grove Street on 30th October but said that there had been another man with Messiter in the garage. The two of them had gone away together leaving Podmore alone, and that was the last time he had seen Messiter. The rest of his statement agreed with what the police already knew – his selling of oil on commission for Messiter (to fictitious addresses as it turned out) and his job at Downton.

The inquest was held on 15th March and the coroner's jury returned an open verdict. The police still did not have enough evidence to charge Podmore with murder – it was all circumstantial. He had, however, confessed to thefts in Manchester, for which he was sentenced to six months in prison. When he was released he was charged with the theft of the wage packets at Downton; he confessed to that and received a further six months. On his release he was then charged with the murder of Messiter, which he strenuously denied, saying that he was a thief but not a murderer.

Podmore was brought to trial on Monday 3rd March 1931 at Winchester Assizes before the Lord Chief Justice himself, Lord Hewart, with the prosecuting counsel Sir Thomas Inskip. Many reporters from the national newspapers were there, as the case had aroused widespread interest. In the court was a model of the garage and yard at Grove Street. The first four days were taken up by the evidence from the prosecution and the defence. Further evidence was given by two prisoners who were with Podmore in Wandsworth prison; they claimed that Podmore had admitted his guilt to them, but in his summing-up Lord Hewart observed that not too much reliance should be placed on that sort of evidence.

On the Friday, Sir Thomas Inskip's final speech took four hours and ten minutes. The defence case rested on Podmore's complete denial of the charge. The reason given for his sudden changes of address and his false name was the attempt to hide from the police after the Manchester swindle and the Downton robbery. Counsel said that there was no direct evidence to incriminate Podmore – the hammer could not be traced to him, there were no bloodstains on his clothes and nothing of Messiter's was found in his possession. The evidence therefore was entirely circumstantial.

The Lord Chief Justice's summing-up lasted three hours and 20 minutes. At the very outset he reminded the jury that the guilt of the accused had to be established beyond a reasonable doubt: 'Not beyond a fantastic, whimsical, or capricious doubt, but such a reasonable doubt as would govern a man's course of action in some private affair of his own.' Having put the minds of the jury at rest on that point (or maybe not!) he examined the evidence. He said that Messiter had been murdered by someone who had locked the doors of the garage after the murder and left everything apparently in order.

He reminded the jury that the evidence was circumstantial

(as indeed the defence counsel had submitted) as distinct from direct evidence, i.e. the evidence of an eyewitness, who could be mistaken or biased. He then gave his own definition of circumstantial evidence: 'Circumstantial evidence consists in this: That when you look at all the surrounding circumstances you find such a series of undesigned, unexpected coincidences that as a reasonable person you find that your judgement is compelled to one conclusion. If the circumstantial evidence is such as to fall short of that standard, if it does not satisfy that test, if it leaves gaps, then it is of no use at all.'

Lord Hewart laid great stress on one piece of evidence, or rather its absence: the missing pages from the books. He argued that if Podmore was indeed the murderer then obviously he would cover his tracks by removing all evidence of written transactions between himself and Messiter. In other words if the murderer was someone other than Podmore, what interest could he have had in destroying Podmore's association with Messiter? He therefore suggested that only Podmore would have removed all such evidence. It does not seem to have occurred to Lord Hewart that a clever murderer would do just that, to throw suspicion on to Podmore.

The jury was convinced by the arguments of Lord Hewart and Sir Thomas Inskip, and after retiring for an hour and 23 minutes returned a verdict of 'Guilty'. Podmore continued to protest his innocence: 'I still repeat, sir, I know nothing whatever about it.' He was sentenced to death and executed at Winchester on 22nd April 1930.

Southampton's Ordeal by Fire

★

On the night of 19th June 1940 Southampton suffered its first air raid. Ten high-explosive bombs fell on Millbrook, causing severe injuries to six people and minor injuries to others, destroying three buildings. The rescue services were so efficient that within 25 minutes all the injured were safely in hospital. One person died of shock during the raid. This was only a foretaste, however, of the battering Southampton was to receive from German bombs later in the year.

Details of all the air raids on Southampton were compiled at the time by ARP workers. They noted the type and number of bombs that fell, where they fell, the number of houses destroyed and damaged, and the number of people killed and injured.

The first deaths caused directly by bombs occurred in the second raid, on the afternoon of 13th August, when 15 bombs were dropped on the town centre and docks and eight on Portswood and Bitterne Park. Six people died and eight buildings were destroyed. When the cold store in the docks was hit and its stock of some 2,300 tons of butter was set on fire it soon became an inferno that millions of gallons of water could not quench and it continued to burn for ten days. In the next big raid, on 11th September when the Battle of Britain raged furiously over England, Southampton airport was the target for 16 bombs. The Cunliffe-Owen aircraft factory was hit and 49 people were killed. Perhaps for security reasons this raid was not reported in the *Southern Daily Echo*.

On the afternoon of 24th September 46 bombs fell on Bitterne, Newtown, Bevois and Northam, causing 42 deaths and damage to nearly 600 buildings. Again this was not reported, but a heavier raid two days later, also in the afternoon, was reported by the *Echo*: 'Fifty 'planes raid on Southampton area'. In Bitterne, Sholing and St Mary's 55 people were killed. The *Echo* said that working-class houses and industrial premises were destroyed. RAF fighters and anti-aircraft guns attacked the German bombers. One man who looked up from under a lorry described seeing a German aircraft blow up – one of its crew fell into the river with his parachute on fire.

The industrial premises referred to by the *Echo* was the Supermarine aircraft factory at Woolston, whose production of Spitfire fighters was vital to the British war effort. The factory was badly damaged but most of the tools and jigs were salvaged; production continued at various sites in Hampshire but it was three months before it was back to normal. The gasworks was hit, disrupting gas supplies for the next eight days. St Barnabas' church and the premises of Hooper and Ashby, the coal merchants at Phoenix Wharf, were also hit.

Tragedy occurred on the afternoon of 6th November when 35 people were killed by 12 bombs ('a rain of bombs' reported the *Echo*). Two of the bombs fell at the Art School in the Civic Centre. One penetrated the shelter and killed several teachers and girls from the Central District Girls School; four girls were brought out alive but only one survived. One class of senior students had not gone to the shelter and so escaped injury. The *Echo* reported that the mayor was among the rescue workers and sadly 'injured his right hand slightly in helping to pull wreckage off the victims'!

Sometimes the *Echo* reports named Southampton as the target of an air raid but occasionally, as on 18th November, said the raid was on 'a South Coast town'. The purpose of

Wartime residents of Southampton go about their daily business, surrounded by devastation.

this anonymity is not clear, as everyone in Southampton was all too aware that there had been a raid. For the first time a large number of incendiary bombs (about 300) were dropped; 55 people were killed and 3,750 buildings destroyed or damaged.

Southampton's three heaviest raids of the war came soon after, the first one on the evening of Saturday 23rd November and the other two a week later. On the 23rd the raid started at 6.40 pm and lasted until 11 pm; about 850 high-explosive bombs and 4,000 incendiaries were dropped on the town centre and its immediate surroundings. Seventy-seven people were killed and more than 300 injured; about 3,500 buildings including shops, banks, cinemas, hotels and public offices were destroyed or damaged. The Civic Centre received direct hits and much of the shopping and business centre of the town was severely damaged. The *Echo* again said the raid was on 'a town on the South Coast' (as did *The Times*); the German radio was more specific, claiming that 250 aircraft had dropped 250 tons of high-explosive bombs on Southampton – the British estimate was 50 tons. Thousands of people were made homeless; some were accommodated in rest centres and others evacuated.

On that Saturday evening the cinemas in the town were crowded when the air raid began. In one cinema most of the audience of 1,500 calmly remained seated when told of the raid, an attitude that is hard to understand today. Even when the programme ended, about 300 people stayed in the cinema until the end of the raid. At another cinema the audience was unaware that incendiary bombs had landed on the roof and had been extinguished by the manager and projectionists.

Two raids on successive evenings came on Saturday 30th November and Sunday 1st December. The first started at 6.25 pm and lasted until 12.30 am and the next day's raid started at 6.15 pm and lasted until 11.30 pm. In those two raids about 800 high-explosive bombs and 9,000 incendiaries fell on the town, killing 137 people and injuring 763. More than 5,800 buildings were destroyed or damaged, many of them in the town centre. The offices of the *Southern Daily Echo* were destroyed but the paper was printed in Bournemouth on the Monday. Its headline that day was: 'Germans' Savage attack on Southampton' and on the Tuesday: 'Salvage day in Stricken Southampton. People Take Stock of All that is left'.

There were many examples of lucky escapes and acts of bravery. For example, the ambulance driven by young Frances Hartley was thrown by the blast of a bomb on to the pavement; seeing three injured men in the road she lifted them into the ambulance and drove to hospital. At the hospital a porter jumped a seven ft gap between the roofs of two buildings to get to an incendiary bomb, throwing it with his bare hands into the street below. It was reported that 674 buildings were on fire at the same time that day.

On the Saturday the furniture store of Mayes and Son was hit within five minutes of the air-raid warning. Incendiary bombs rained on the town for several hours, interspersed with high-explosive bombs. The town centre became an inferno of fire, with intermittent blasts of hot air and debris from the explosions. Although the Air Ministry communiqué stated 'All fires are under control', this eventually became impossible. Most of the water mains damaged on 23rd November had been repaired but were soon put out of action again.

Reinforcements of 2,000 firemen and 160 fire-engines arrived, some from as far away as Oxford and Reading, but there was not enough water for them to use, and some of their equipment would not fit on the Southampton hydrants. Water was pumped from the Electricity Department cooling pond and until the tide went out, from Town Quay. Some was carried from the Common reservoirs until they ran dry. As a result many buildings were still burning when the second raid began and the water shortage became even more acute. The deficiencies of the Southampton fire service were commented on by the firemen from outside – no fire-fighting towers, no static water-tanks and rotten hosepipes. Not long afterwards the Southampton Chief Fire Officer was awarded the CBE.

At daybreak on the Monday the centre of Southampton was a scene of devastation. Much of it was in ruins, the streets littered with bricks, concrete and glass; many buildings were still on fire. Those shops that had survived somehow managed to open for business; among those destroyed were Plummer Roddis, Edwin Jones and Woolworth's. Holy Rood church was destroyed and St Mary's church was gutted – services continued in its roofless nave. A single van with a barely audible

Anderson shelters, cold and damp and initially despised, saved hundreds of lives.

loudspeaker advised people to boil their tap water and to take advantage of the free inoculation against typhoid.

Much of the town centre had ceased to exist. Seven Anglican churches and seven churches of other denominations, including the Above Bar Congregational church, were destroyed. The telephone exchange had been hit, so communications in the town were either verbal or non-existent. To make matters worse, at the height of the Sunday raid most of the Army's dispatch riders were withdrawn from Southampton to take part in military exercises. The Army telephones at Bassett House were commandeered in order to communicate with the outside world. The massive medieval gateway, the Bargate, was unscathed but it would have required a direct hit to have made any impression on it. As Southampton's town centre was not so densely populated, there were fewer deaths than in places such as Coventry and Portsmouth.

On 5th December King George VI paid a visit to Southampton Civic Centre accompanied by Herbert Morrison, the Minister of Home Security. It was the King's fourth visit to the Centre: In 1930 when Duke of York he laid its foundation stone, in 1932 he officially opened the building and in 1939 was received there on his return from Canada and the USA. This time he also visited the docks, crossed the river by the floating bridge and made an unscheduled visit to Woolston fire station.

On the same day the Government's Inspector-General of Air Raid Precautions visited Southampton to assess the situation. In his report (released in 1973) he severely criticized the town clerk, who had been the ARP Controller ('entirely unsuitable'), the Regional Controller (for lack of support), and the mayor (for leaving the town every afternoon with the general exodus of people seeking safety in the countryside). The Council denied the allegations; the Government accepted its protest and altered the Inspector-General's report accordingly.

The report caused angry protests in Southampton, as did the report by Mass Observation released at the same time, which said that morale had deteriorated to the point where people felt that Southampton was finished because so little had been done to rally local feeling. The Bishop of Winchester had found the people 'broken in spirit – everywhere there was fear'. The report said that the obsessive talk about the air raids was becoming a neurosis, and that the failure and disorganization of the local authorities was the talk of the county.

We are in no position to criticize the Southampton people for their reaction to this terrible ordeal, when today whole areas of a town are cleared for one suspected terrorist bomb. The response to the bombing was the same as in other towns in England and lack of civic leadership was commonplace. The fault lay in the planning by the ARP authorities, which was directed towards dealing with bombs rather than with a disoriented and homeless population.

Thousands of people left the town every afternoon by car, bus and train and on foot to sleep with friends (if lucky) or in barns and fields (if unlucky), returning the next morning. The natural desire not to be killed was frowned upon by authority, who referred to them as 'trekkers'. The official decision to refuse aid to those who were not actually homeless did nothing to improve their morale – there was little food in the shops and for the majority, no gas, electricity, water or telephone.

Southampton suffered intermittent raids throughout 1941, the worst on 8th July when in a raid in the early hours 150 high-explosive bombs and 5,000 incendiaries fell on the town, killing 38 people. Two churches, several schools and two banks were damaged. During the air raids in Southampton the Anderson shelters saved hundreds of lives; time after time a bomb exploding only a few yards from one had left the occupants uninjured. Only a direct hit seemed to affect them, so impregnable were they.

The last serious raid of the war occurred on 22nd June 1942, when 4,000 incendiaries were dropped within an hour and a half. Thirty-six people died and 2,800 buildings were destroyed or damaged. The *Echo*, reverting again to anonymity, reported that 'neighbouring towns in a southern area' were raided. (Eastleigh was the other one.) *The Times* and the Air Ministry both named Southampton as the target. The last air-raid warning of the war came on 5th November 1944.

In the four years from 1940 to 1944, 2,631 high-explosive bombs (475 tons) and more than 30,000 incendiaries were dropped on Southampton in nearly 70 air raids. Deaths totalled 631 and 1,888 people were injured, 903 of them seriously; 936 buildings were completely destroyed, another 2,653 had to be demolished and another 40,946 were damaged in some way. The air-raid sirens sounded more than 1,600 times. The people of Southampton had suffered an ordeal by fire, bomb and deprivation never likely to be repeated.

The Winter of Our Discontent

★

The first half of January 1947 had been stormy and wet and the weather was abnormally mild. Saturday 18th January, however, proved to be the last mild day for nearly two months, during which time the people of Great Britain, already enduring the bleak austerity of the post-war years, suffered a terrible ordeal by cold weather. Snow fell in Kent on Thursday 23rd January and after two days respite spread to other parts of the country. The snow then fell for 24 hours, a gale-force east wind piling it into enormous drifts, the temperature falling to 12° F – 20 degrees of frost. Few people, least of all the Meteorological Office, imagined that the snow would be with them for the next two months.

For prolonged unpleasantness the weather from then until mid-March exceeded anything in living memory. People were unable to heat their houses for lack of fuel, and there was an almost complete absence of sunshine. In that 1947 winter the sun was rarely seen, certainly not in the first three weeks of February, the longest 'sunless' period ever recorded in Great Britain.

Worst of all was the succession of blizzards, driven along by gales. The whole country was covered with snow from 27th January to mid-March, and every day between 23rd January and 17th March snow fell somewhere in Great Britain. Early in February England was divided into two parts, north and south of a line from the Mersey to the Humber, and snow drifts made road communication between them impossible. By March the snow was two ft deep over much of the country and drifts of ten ft and over were quite common.

Wednesday 29th January was the coldest night for many years in England. At midnight Big Ben struck one instead of 12, the striking mechanism affected by frost. The *Hampshire Chronicle* reported that the heaviest snowfall in the county for many years had occurred on Thursday 30th January and that the temperature on 29th January in Winchester had fallen to 1° F – 31 degrees of frost. Water supplies were frozen and many schools in Hampshire had to close. One firm of plumbers received nearly 100 calls on that Thursday alone. In some parts of the county there were power shortages.

The AA, in a unique understatement, said that road conditions were 'generally bad'. Snow-ploughs were out throughout the county attempting to clear the roads 'without serving any very useful purpose', and gangs of workmen cleared pavements. A squad of policemen pushed cars up Romsey Road; small children watching their efforts had a good laugh when the policemen regularly lost their balance and fell. On the Winchester to Chandler's Ford road and the Winchester to Wickham road the snow was a foot deep.

People were soon out skating on the moors at Winnall and they were tobogganing on St Catherine's Hill and Teg Down. Farms experienced difficulties with milk collection and with new-born lambs. Curiously, there were fewer twin lambs born than usual, perhaps as a result of the severe cold. Observant people remarked on the absence of birds, which obviously suffered acutely in the severe frost.

On 8th and 9th February another ten inches of snow fell in the south-eastern counties and Hampshire. The temperature remained below freezing night and day throughout the following two weeks. In the middle of this longest 'sunless' period on record the film at Winchester Odeon was *Blue Skies*. On 20th February heavy snow fell in the West Country and spread to the rest of England over the next two days. Sheet ice formed in Southampton Water, holding fast many small boats. For most of that two months there was frost; between 11th and 23rd February it was continuous, night and day. Worse, a sub-zero east wind blew for a whole month, from the onset of the snow until 22nd February.

As a reminder that winter was not yet over, the worst storm of all hit the south Midlands and north Hampshire on 4th March, with 12 inches of snow and drifts up to 30 ft deep, blocking all roads between the Midlands and the south. Before this latest storm there had been rain, turning to sleet, which froze and formed a thick coat of ice on roads, trees and telephone wires. The ice stayed for several days and was so bad that men could not climb the telephone poles to carry out repairs and many lines and exchanges were out of action. Ice on the rails delayed electric trains to London from the south for several hours and they had to be assisted by steam engines. In the Owslebury and Sutton Scotney areas 50% of the telephone wires were down.

In normal times people would have struggled through such a winter, keeping themselves warm by their fires. But these were not normal times. Coinciding with this abominable weather, and partly caused by it, was an acute shortage of coal. Never before in Great Britain had a cold winter been accompanied by a fuel shortage and this was the worst winter of the century. By January, house coal was in desperately short supply, and the public was only now becoming aware of the seriousness of the situation caused by the Government's failure in 1946 to foresee the impending shortage of coal.

In 1947, when the coal industry was nationalized, over 90% of the country's total heat, light and power came from British coal. By early January coal and electricity supplies were falling and gas supplies threatened, causing disruption to industry long before the severe weather arrived. The gravity of the situation was such that even Emanuel

Shinwell, the Minister of Fuel and Power, now admitted that there was a crisis.

British industries normally used about 1,000,000 tons of coal per week but on 20th January supplies (except those to the iron and steel industry) were cut by half, three days before the real winter began. Domestic users received about three-quarters of their normal requirements, but because of the severe weather this reduction inflicted considerable hardship. In February stocks of coal at power stations and gasworks were so low that cuts in electricity and gas supplies were imminent. The Ministry of Fuel and Power warned that future supplies of coal could not be guaranteed. The arrival of the snow brought chaos to London's coal supplies; hitherto the shortage had been felt mainly in the north of England. To cap it all a strike by road-haulage drivers threatened to halt food supplies over a wide area, causing the Labour Government reluctantly to bring in troops.

The initial shortage of coal was not caused by the weather, but snow and frost made distribution of the supplies that were available much more difficult – transport of coal in some areas was virtually impossible. Road, rail and sea transport were disrupted throughout February, a vicious circle as far as the railways were concerned because they were not getting enough coal to run the trains that carried the coal.

Early in February, Hampshire coal merchants announced that customers would receive no more than two cwt for the rest of the month, unless they had no other means of cooking; in that case they would receive one cwt per week. Schools in the county were given priority and they were even able to provide meals for their pupils, although some of them had to resort to burning packing-cases. A shortage of fuel closed the Portal paper mill at Overton for a week. At Basingstoke and Alton the shops had to use various kinds of temporary heating such as oil and paraffin lamps and candles. But coke, a by-product of the coal used by the gas companies, was available in some towns for those who had the means of collecting it from their local gasworks.

From 10th February electricity supplies to households in London and the south-east, the Midlands and the north-west were cut off from 9 am to 12 noon and from 2 pm to 4 pm every day; later these cuts were applied to the whole country, and people were asked to exercise restraint outside these hours. Essential services were not affected by the cuts; these included hospitals, transport, food factories and bakeries (and the Houses of Parliament!). To set an example the BBC television service and radio Third Programme closed down. Newspapers were reduced in size and many magazines were told to cease publication for the time being (in fact, only two weeks as it turned out).

Street lights, advertising signs and shop-window lights were immediately banned. 'Unnecessary' consumers of electricity, such as greyhound-racing tracks, were not allowed to operate. Restaurants cooking by electricity could do so only from 12 noon to 2 pm, and cinemas and theatres were allowed to open only after 4 pm. Those people whose electricity supplies were not cut because they lived near essential services were first asked to make a voluntary cut, then from 13th February were penalised for not doing so. After one week of these restrictions consumption of coal by power stations had fallen by 35% and continued to fall, but at a reduced rate. By 8th March the fuel position in Winchester was said to be one of 'unrelieved gloom'.

On 15th March the Winchester Fuel Advisory Committee issued the following notice:

'Supplies of coal in Winchester and District are critical in the extreme. There is insufficient coal available to permit of any deliveries except:
1. To householders who depend solely on coal for cooking.

93

2. In response to really urgent medical certificates.
What is left will be allocated to those households which
have had no deliveries since 28th February. Under no
circumstances will a delivery be made even under the
above headings to a household which has any stock of
fuel.'

There was no definition of 'really urgent' medical certificates
– presumably they were those for people at death's door. By
15th March, however, the winter was nearly over, and coal
production and its transport almost back to normal, so why
there was such a shortage in Hampshire remains a mystery.
But the local coal merchants did their best for their
customers, even resorting to Sunday deliveries.

The main result of all these restrictions and prohibitions
was a startling rise in unemployment, from 400,000 in
January to 2,500,000 in late February, with another 500,000
not working but receiving wages. By then living conditions
were grim – high unemployment, uncertain deliveries of
mail, shortages of milk and coal, biting winds and freezing
houses, many of which were without coal for weeks on end.
Hypothermia took a deadly toll of old people – their
mortality rate was 18% higher than normal for the time of
year. The Government received most of the blame,
especially Emanuel Shinwell, for the coal shortage if not for
the weather. Shinwell received harsh criticism for his
unwarranted optimism about the position of coal stocks at
the end of 1946.

From the start of the coal crisis householders had switched
to gas and electricity. In response to this excessive demand
the power stations resorted to load-shedding and shut-
downs. As these increased in frequency those households
that had been persuaded to rely exclusively on electricity for
all their heating, lighting and cooking were in great
difficulties.

Life for the great majority of people was even harder than

during the war. For many there was no work, no fuel and little money (the old age pension was less than £1) and rationing was still in force. Bread, in unrestricted supply during the war, was now rationed. In many ways it was just like wartime – rationing, austerity and no street lighting. One of the most alarming reports was of dwindling stocks of beer, and that parts of the country looked like becoming 'dry' for a few weeks!

By the end of February coal production was at a record level and transport, especially by rail, was getting back to normal. On 10th March a thaw came to southern England, accompanied by winds of up to 100 mph, followed by heavy rain. In Winchester three inches fell in one week, including an inch in one night alone. At Romsey, the Tadburn overflowed and formed a lake in Botley Road. The river Meon was unrecognizable, its real course hidden by sheets of water covering the valley. This March turned out to be the wettest on record, and April was little better, all this rain and melting snow inevitably resulting in the worst river floods for 50 years, affecting 31 counties.

The effect on winter crops was disastrous, many being ruined, and spring sowing was found to be impossible. Hayrick fires, caused by internal combustion, became commonplace, the stacks having been gathered wet in the autumn. Three hayricks at Botley and six at Durley caught fire.

The frost had been so severe and had penetrated so deep that the thaw took a long time; the rain simply ran off the fields. Road surfaces in Hampshire deteriorated alarmingly, especially those on the chalk. Minor roads were badly affected by pot-holes and travelling around the county entailed a series of diversions or 'one-ways' until repairs could be completed.

The beleaguered British people, already hardened by the war years, had stoically endured the hardships of the 1947 winter, but it was one that few would ever forget.

Tragedy Over Farnborough

★

On the afternoon of Saturday 6th September 1952 a vast crowd, estimated at 125,000, waited silently and expectantly at Farnborough airfield, their eyes focussed on a patch of blue sky immediately above them. No one suspected that they were about to witness a re-enactment of a 39 year old tragedy, one that was to have even more horrific consequences.

The occasion was the 13th Air Show organized by the Society of British Aircraft Constructors, the fifth time it had been held at Farnborough. The first was held in 1932 at Hendon, then at Hatfield and Radlett before moving to Farnborough in 1948. Although it could not accommodate as many spectators as other airfields, Farnborough was the birthplace of British aviation and therefore an appropriate home for the country's most important air display. Here in October 1908 Samuel Cody made the first officially recognized aeroplane flight in Great Britain, here the Royal Engineers Air Battalion was formed and here the first military flying trials were held.

The first British aircraft exhibition was held at Olympia in 1909, only a few months after Cody's record flight and before Blériot had flown across the English Channel. Only one of the eleven aircraft on display had actually flown! Cody, an American who became a naturalized British subject in 1912, experimented over the next few years with aeroplanes of his own design, achieving ever longer and faster flights. He was brought up on a Texas ranch and his skills as a horseman and marksman seemed more appropriate to a cowboy than to an aviator, yet he became an

The remains of the hydro-biplane, the largest aeroplane Cody had built, which crumpled and crashed in mid-flight killing Cody and his passenger.

expert mechanic and designer of aircraft. He perfected a man-lifting kite, flew his own airship over London in 1907, won the 1912 Military Trials Competition and was awarded the Royal Aero Club Gold Medal.

In August 1913 the airfield at Farnborough was then the site of the Royal Aircraft Factory. Cody was testing an aeroplane designed and built by himself, a hydro-biplane with a 100 hp Green engine. Of wooden construction covered with fabric, it was the largest aeroplane he had ever built and had a maximum speed of 70 mph. He had entered it for the 1913 Circuit of Britain race, for the £5,000 *Daily Mail* prize. In this race round the coast, starting from Calshot, Hampshire, his aircraft would be fitted with floats, but here on trial it had a wheel-and-skid undercarriage.

On the morning of 7th August Cody had taken his aeroplane for a trial flight and was about to take off again with his son Leon as passenger when, by chance, W H B Evans, the former Hampshire county cricketer, arrived and after introducing himself, persuaded Cody to take him up instead. All seemed well as the aircraft took off and headed across the plain towards Bramshott golf course at a height variously estimated by witnesses as between 100 and 500 ft. It turned and was over Ball Hill near Cove Common heading back towards Cody's shed when suddenly it crumpled up and started to fall. The pilot and his passenger fell to the ground and were killed instantly, while the aircraft fell into a clump of trees.

The Army signallers who witnessed the accident said that it all happened within a few seconds; to another witness the engine appeared to stop without warning, the wings folded like the closing of a book and the passengers were catapulted forwards out of the aircraft. A police constable reported that the bottom part of the machine seemed to detach itself from the rest, and the tail shot up and 'flapped about'. A 14 year old girl who was near the spot saw the aeroplane turn to start its return journey, then '[it] broke into a hundred pieces and a man fell out' when it was just above the level of the trees.

That same day Cody was to have flown the aircraft to Calshot to have floats fitted. On the Wednesday he had been to Calshot by road with the floats, and had said how optimistic he was of his chances of winning the big race. He had even talked of flying the Atlantic in 1914 in a triplane fitted with his own 500 hp engine.

At the inquest Leon Cody testified that his father and Evans had not been strapped in the aircraft – his father never liked to be strapped in. He suggested that perhaps the propeller had burst and damaged the top wing, but there was no way of checking that, because the pieces of the propeller were missing, possibly taken by souvenir hunters.

The Royal Aero Club said that the aircraft's fall had been broken by the trees, so the part of the fuselage in which Cody and Evans had been sitting was not greatly damaged. The Club was of the opinion that if they had been strapped in they might well have survived the crash; there were several cases of pilots escaping comparatively unhurt after their aircraft had fallen into trees. The cause of the crash was put down to inherent structural weakness, and it ended the career of the most flamboyant of early aviators. Cody had died as he would have wished – flying his own aeroplane. A crowd of 100,000 people lined the route of his funeral procession when he was buried in the Military Cemetery at Aldershot.

In 1952 at Farnborough, 39 years after that fatal crash, aircraft of a design and performance that Cody could never have imagined were being put through their paces. The star performer was undoubtedly the Avro 698 delta-wing bomber, powered by four Rolls-Royce engines, which had flown for the first time only a few days before the show. Other newcomers were the giant Bristol Britannia airliner, the Hawker Hunter fighter and the Saunders-Roe Princess flying boat, built at colossal expense and first launched and flown that summer.

The aircraft the spectators now awaited so eagerly was also a newcomer to the show. One of two prototypes that had been built, the de Havilland 110 fighter 40,000 ft above them had been flown for a total of 125 hours since its first flight in September 1951. On 9th April 1952 it had become the first two-seater aircraft to exceed the speed of sound, a feat it had repeated more than 100 times since then. It was an unusual twin-boom design and was powered by two Rolls-Royce axial-flow turbo-jet engines. The pilot was 30 year old John Derry, de Havilland's chief test pilot, who by a coincidence four years previously to the very day had become the first airman to exceed the speed of sound in Great Britain, in the de Havilland 108 research aircraft. He was accompanied now by Anthony Richards, the flight test observer.

Because of protests from local residents there had been a ban on supersonic speeds on the first two days of the show but on the Wednesday Derry had successfully flown the 110 through the sound barrier. The prototype aircraft (WG240) that Derry had used on the previous five days of the show, which had first flown on 25th July 1952, had developed a fault and so today he had brought the other one (WG236) from Hatfield. Everybody assumed that the two aircraft were identical − but they were not.

A tiny silver speck suddenly appeared in the blue sky heading in a dive towards the airfield, soon followed by two puffs of smoke and the sound of a double bang or boom, the

A huge crowd lined the route of Cody's funeral procession; this larger than life figure had caught the public imagination.

usual noise made by an aircraft breaking the sound barrier. The aircraft continued its dive, levelled out at about 1,500 ft over the airfield, then made a high-speed run above the main runway at about 50-100 ft, leaving the spectators gasping in astonishment.

Derry then turned the aircraft to the north of Farnborough and approached the airfield over Cove radio station for a second high-speed run, heading towards Cove Hill at a height of about 500 ft. He was then, by an eerie coincidence, close to the same flight path taken by Cody 39 years ago on his last tragic trip. The aircraft, seemingly under perfect control, had reached a point about one mile outside the perimeter of the airfield, and about one mile and a half from the public enclosures, when without warning its nose tilted and the aircraft completely disintegrated. There was no explosion – one moment it was flying steadily, the next moment pieces of it were falling to the ground. The two engines broke loose from the fuselage and hurtled on at high speed towards the public enclosures.

Few witnesses afterwards could describe accurately the exact sequence of events. Fred Jones, the accident investigator, examined 1,200 statements and hundreds of photographs from witnesses and found that less than a dozen statements tallied with the actual sequence of events when he later pieced them together. So much for eyewitness accounts. Even cine-cameras were not fast enough to record the details of the aircraft's disintegration, so quickly did it happen.

As Mrs Derry watched from the pilots' enclosure, the aeroplane broke up. The agitated voice of the announcer was heard over the loudspeakers. 'My God! Look out! Look out!' But there was no time for anyone to move. As the engines passed over their heads the spectators ducked and tried to run but in a matter of seconds the engines had plunged to the ground. One had hurtled into the spectators gathered on Observation Hill, a low mound close to the main runway that offered a good viewpoint for the day's display. Closely packed shoulder to shoulder, they were unable to move out of the way of the deadly missile, which scythed its way through them, inflicting terrible injuries. For a few moments there was silence as the uninjured stood stunned by the catastrophe, while wisps of blue smoke rose from the wreckage.

Ambulances and fire-engines were soon at the scene. Some spectators covered the dead with their coats and gave help to the injured. There was no panic, but hundreds of people started to leave the airfield. A lone helicopter hovered above the scene and directed the rescue operation. The other engine had fortunately missed the spectators; one witness said that it fell on open ground, another that it fell through the roof of a hangar. Part of the fuselage with the cockpit landed near the edge of the main runway, causing further injuries to spectators.

Apart from the engine that caused most of the casualties, eight other pieces of the aircraft fell among the crowd. Thirty people, including the pilot and observer, were killed and many more injured. Some of the dead were so terribly mutilated that they could be identified only by their clothing or personal papers. The rescue services were so efficient that all the casualties had been taken to hospital within an hour of the accident. After a short interval the air display continued with Neville Duke breaking the sound barrier in the Hawker Hunter.

Three Winchester visitors, one of them an eleven year old boy, told how they had moved down the hill to get a better view only half an hour before the tragedy. They said there was a deathly hush as the engine flew towards them; they dropped to the ground and when they got up saw that they were only six ft from the crater caused by the engine. A visitor from Southampton described how the fuselage fell to the ground 30 yards from him as he dodged falling fragments. One man and his six-year-old son were so close to the spot where the engine landed that they were covered in blood from those who were killed. Another man felt the heat of the aircraft's nose as it narrowly missed him and saw it explode as it hit the ground.

Mr V Gardner, the secretary of the Farnborough and RAE Camera Club, filmed the accident from start to finish. He said that the fuselage and tail booms had 'swooped towards him' as he stood with his camera aimed at the wreckage. He had been filming the aircraft when he saw pieces of it fly off, and he continued to film the various parts as they fell, one piece as it was coming straight towards him. His dramatic pictures were printed in the local newspaper.

A man from Weybridge was standing about 100 yards from the perimeter fence when the aircraft 'just seemed to fall apart; something small fell off first, and then the main body fell to the ground'. One large piece landed 100 yards from him. Another man from Aldershot, who was watching through binoculars, said that 'pieces of the aeroplane seemed to break away and fall through the air like paper.' One of the injured was a 13 year old boy in the front row of the enclosure. He was lucky that he had put on his wellingtons that day because although his right leg was broken by a splinter from the wreckage the boots undoubtedly saved him from more serious injury.

Group Captain Hughes, who had been supervising the flying programme from the control tower, told the inquest that Derry had informed him over the radio telephone that he had started his supersonic dive at 3.46 pm and that there was no further message from the pilot except an acknowledgement ('Roger') that the sonic bang had been heard on the airfield. He was convinced that Derry had had no warning that the aircraft was about to break up. It appeared to have just straightened out of a turn when it disintegrated.

When all the parts had been recovered Fred Jones began the search for the cause of the break-up. He soon narrowed

A local example of the extensive news coverage of the 1913 Cody disaster.

it down to the wings and then worked out the cause of the disaster. He deduced that when Derry pulled out of his turn to straighten up for his second high-speed run and started to climb to gain extra height, the pulling back of the control column together with the raising of the starboard aileron (a hinged flap near the wing tips) would have introduced 'g'-loading in the wing structure. This loading had caused the leading edge of the starboard wing to buckle at the point where the outer part of the wing joined the strengthened inner part. The wing had been torn off like a piece of paper, and a chain reaction had detached the other wing, the engines and the fuselage. The aircraft had disintegrated in less than a second.

Then Jones made an important discovery. Both prototype 110s had been provided with an aerodynamic 'fence' on the outside leading edge of each wing, at the precise point where this one had buckled, as a method of varying the airflow over the wing when under test. The prototype 110 WG240, which had been declared unserviceable that Saturday, had its fence in place, but on the one flown that fateful day (WG236), the fence had been removed as part of the test programme. The fence, whose purpose was ostensibly to deal with airflow over the wing, had provided external stiffening and had prevented the wing from buckling. But fence or no fence, the under-stressed wing was sure to have failed sooner or later when subjected to high-speed manoeuvres. It had lasted this long only because of the fence, and poor Derry did not know that once the fence had been removed, he was flying a potential death-trap. Design weakness had apparently been suspected, but the Controller of Aircraft had been persuaded to let the 110 appear at the show.

Jones's theory was proved correct when a non-flying DH 110 was given a structural test at Hatfield. When the loading and pressure conditions prevailing at the moment of disaster were simulated on a test rig, the wing buckled at the precise spot that he had anticipated. He must have had mixed feelings at that moment – pleasure in the knowledge that he had been proved right but sadness at the thought that had certain precautions been taken, a terrible air disaster might never have happened.

The Mystery of the Missing Frogman

★

When John Randall, fishing in Chichester Harbour on Sunday 9th June 1957, found the headless body of a man in a frogman's suit, he little realised that another chapter in a 14 month old mystery was about to begin. After examination by the local police and RAF officers the body was taken to Chichester mortuary, where the pathologist was unable to establish the cause of death and the body could not be identified. Who was he?

The local police superintendent voiced the suspicion, which had already occurred to several people, that the body was that of Commander Lionel Crabb, the ex-Navy frogman who had gone missing more than a year ago, but Mrs Crabb could not identify the body as that of her ex-husband. According to Lieutenant McLanachan, an expert on diving gear, the frogman's suit was not Admiralty standard issue. The inquest on the Tuesday lasted less than two minutes and was postponed for a fortnight while further information was sought.

When the inquest was resumed on 26th June the pathologist said that the body had been in the sea for at least six months and possibly for 14 months. It had not been possible to determine the cause of death. He said that the big toes were deformed and that there was a scar on the left knee, both features Crabb was known to have, thus contradicting his statement at the mortuary that he could see no toe deformity or scar (nor could Mrs Crabb). The coroner was convinced that the body was that of Commander Crabb, even though there was nothing that could positively identify him. He suggested that various coincidences – size of feet and legs, toe deformity, scar on the knee and frogman's distinctive suit – together added up to only one conclusion. But others were not so convinced and speculation continued about the true fate of Commander Crabb.

Commander Lionel Crabb OBE GM RNVR was probably the most experienced frogman in the world; his many daring exploits during and after the Second World War had made him famous. He had worked as a mine and bomb-disposal officer, and in 1943 was responsible for keeping the ports in north Italy clear of mines during the Allied invasion. After the war he was often called upon for special assignments, such as locating the submarine HMS *Truculent* when it sank at the mouth of the Thames. Crabb was a brave and often reckless character whose skill as a frogman made him at the age of 46 the leading expert on underwater warfare.

The public first became aware that Crabb was missing and presumed dead when his obituary appeared in *The Times* on 30th April 1956, the day after the Admiralty stated that his death had been presumed after 'trials with certain underwater apparatus in Stokes Bay'. He had been reported missing on Friday 20th April after diving in Portsmouth Harbour early the previous morning. It was perhaps no coincidence that the Soviet cruiser *Ordzhonikidze* and two destroyers were in dock there after having brought the Russian leaders Bulganin and Krushchev on a visit to England. Two naval officers had seen Crabb enter the water in his frogman's suit near the Sallyport and swim in the direction of the Russian warships. That was the last time anybody in England saw Crabb alive.

The newspapers began to speculate on what had really happened to Crabb in Portsmouth Harbour, coming up with some fanciful stories, the most popular of which were that he had been caught and killed by the Russians while spying underneath the *Ordzhonikidze*, that he had been captured and

The charismatic Commander Crabb — the mystery surrounding his disappearance in Portsmouth Harbour in 1956 remains unsolved.

taken back to Russia, and that he had been accidentally killed and his body secretly buried to avoid awkward questions.

On 4th May the Soviet embassy in London sent a note to the British Foreign Office asking why a frogman had been near the Russian ships. The British reply a few days later admitted that the frogman seen by Russian sailors was 'to all appearances' Commander Crabb but that he was there without the permission of the British Government, who expressed regret over the incident.

The next move was a statement in the House of Commons on 9th May by the Prime Minister, Sir Anthony Eden, in reply to a question from John Dugdale, a member of the Opposition. He said that it was not in the public interest to disclose the circumstances in which Crabb had died, that 'what had been done' was without the authority or knowledge of the Government, and that 'appropriate disciplinary steps' were being taken. Hugh Gaitskell, Leader of the Opposition, was not satisfied with this answer and suggested that the Government was trying to hide a 'very grave blunder'. The Prime Minister declined to elaborate on his statement when Gaitskell asked whether anyone was guilty of espionage during the Russian visit. Many Members thought the reference to 'disciplinary steps' was tactless as it led only to speculation about the culpability of someone in authority.

The newspapers unearthed more evidence concerning Crabb's movements prior to his disappearance. He had stayed for one night at the Sallyport Hotel with a 'Mr Smith', who had taken away both his and Crabb's belongings and paid their bills on the Thursday. The police had visited the hotel and torn out the page of the register containing their names. If the purpose of this was to remove evidence that Crabb had been in Portsmouth it was proved pointless by the Government's admission of Crabb's presence there. Perhaps the page was taken to study the handwriting.

In the House of Commons on 14th May the Prime Minister made a short statement about the Crabb case but refused to amplify his statement of the previous week. He deplored the action of the Opposition in taking the debate to a vote (won by the Government by 316 votes to 229). He would say no more about Crabb because it might have jeopardised the outcome of the talks with Russia, and in any case he could not answer the Labour Party without disclosing secret matters. The Opposition concluded that the reluctance to give further information was proof that the Government was covering up Admiralty incompetence.

A month later a German newspaper added a bizarre twist to the story by claiming that Crabb was a prisoner in Russia, reporting the remark made at a banquet by a Soviet officer to a French politician: 'We have got Crabb.' In case the Frenchman thought he was referring to the menu the Russian had added 'He is our prisoner.' The newspaper devoted a whole page to the story. The Soviet officer had defended his country's right to arrest a spy in the 'extra-territorial waters' around the Soviet warships adding that Crabb had been offered a ten year post in the Soviet navy with a promise that he would not be involved in anti-British espionage. This story was no doubt embroidered by the Russian, the Frenchman and the newspaper but, however unlikely, there may have been some truth in it. If indeed he had been captured Crabb perhaps would have been faced with the choice of the job he loved or execution for spying.

A year later the headless and handless body of a frogman was found in Chichester Harbour. Was it a coincidence that Soviet submarines had passed through the English Channel only three days before its discovery? At the inquest why did the pathologist change his mind about the evidence of the toes and the scar? Why was Lieutenant McLanachan not called to give evidence about the diving suit? Why was no comment made on the missing head and hands – surely a strange feature? Was the head removed perhaps by whoever

111

put the body in the sea to prevent positive identification?

The official story ended with the burial of 'Commander Crabb' at Milton cemetery on 5th July 1957. But it was not the end of the unofficial stories, which continued to hit the newspaper headlines from time to time. All the stories, messages and 'evidence' that appeared in the next year or so were described as nonsense by the British and Russian Governments; as far as they were concerned Crabb was dead and buried and nothing would ever alter that. But was he?

The most convincing piece of evidence was a copy of a secret dossier, allegedly smuggled out of Russia, sent to the *Evening News* in November 1959. It contained the full report and details of all that was supposed to have occurred from the time the Soviet warships arrived at Portsmouth on 18th April 1956 to the recruitment of Crabb into the Soviet navy. A book *Frogman Extraordinary* by J Bernard Hutton based on this secret dossier aroused great interest and controversy. Questions were asked in the House of Commons but the Foreign Secretary, Selwyn Lloyd, stated that he had no further information (or if he had he declined to give it).

The next piece of 'evidence', sent by an underground movement in Russia, was a photograph of one Lieutenant Korablov of the Soviet navy. Mrs Crabb identified the man as her ex-husband, as did several other people who had known him well. The *People*, however, claimed that the picture was a fake. The *News of the World*, under the headline 'Frogman Crabb is alive', reported that Commander Kerans MP (famous as the commander of HMS *Amethyst* in China in 1949) was convinced that Crabb was alive in Russia. The Chichester police, the coroner and the pathologist, all of whom apparently had been satisfied that the body was that of Crabb, declined to comment on the dossier.

The arguments continued. Some of Crabb's friends believed he was dead, some that he was alive in Russia. Whatever the Government secretly knew, it maintained that his body was in Milton cemetery and that the dossier and photograph were fakes. But people with long experience of the Communist world believed that they were genuine. Reports about the activities of Crabb in the Soviet navy continued to be received.

A more convincing statement from nearer home came from Sir Percy Sillitoe, former head of MI5. He believed that the dossier was genuine because an identical dossier had been obtained by his organisation. The two naval officers who had witnessed Crabb slip into the harbour that fateful morning were again interviewed. This time they testified that after a struggle in the water Crabb had been taken aboard the Soviet cruiser.

In 1962 an 'official' statement was 'leaked' to the West by the Russian authorities. For the first time it was admitted that Crabb had served in the Soviet navy as Lieutenant Korablov but had recently been killed in an accident. But this report was not accepted as genuine, nor was an alleged eyewitness account of the kidnapping which later emerged from Estonia.

Was Crabb captured in Portsmouth Harbour? The Soviet Government would not have admitted that a British subject had been kidnapped in British territorial waters, nor would the British Government admit that a British frogman had been officially spying on Soviet ships. If he was not captured but killed, by accident or otherwise, why did his body take so long to be found? Commander Kerans pointed out that the prevailing currents could not have taken his body to the spot where it was found.

Why were the head and hands missing from the body? If, as the Government alleged, Crabb died while on underwater trials, why was there no attempt to find his body? Was it found and hidden for security reasons? Until the Russian or British Government cares to shed more light on the case, the fate of Commander Lionel Crabb will remain a mystery.

Pompey's Glory

★

The clouds of war were already gathering over Europe when on Saturday 29th April 1939 the two teams representing Portsmouth Football Club and Wolverhampton Wanderers Football Club ran on to the pitch at Wembley Stadium to contest the FA Cup Final. The storm was destined to break only four months later, but on this day the entire football world had its eyes and ears fixed on Wembley.

For Portsmouth it was their third appearance in the final at Wembley, having been the losing team in 1929 and 1934. For Wolverhampton ('Wolves' for short), it was their sixth appearance in the final but their first at Wembley. They had previously won the Cup in 1893 (at Fallowfield, Manchester) and in 1908 (at Crystal Palace).

Portsmouth Football Club was founded in April 1898 when six businessmen met to raise nearly £5,000 to purchase five acres of land, on which was built Fratton Park. Portsmouth entered the Southern League in 1899, finished second in their first season and became champions at the end of the 1901-2 season. In their last season in the Southern League they were champions again before joining the Third Division (South) when it was founded in 1920. They gained promotion to the Second Division in 1924 and to the First Division in 1927, the first club from the Southern League to do so. They had remained there ever since (and were destined to stay there until relegated in 1959).

In the 1929 final, Portsmouth faced Bolton Wanderers, winners in 1923 of the first final ever held at Wembley. Portsmouth escaped relegation in 1929 by only a few points, finishing 20th in the League. While they were bottom of the

League they had beaten Aston Villa 1-0 in the Cup semifinal at Highbury. The allocation of Cup Final tickets was even more contentious in 1929 than it is today. Portsmouth were given only 3,750 out of 92,000 who watched the game. In contrast to today's media coverage the Football Association refused the BBC permission to broadcast the game. Bolton won but left it late, scoring twice in the last 12 minutes after the Portsmouth left-back had been injured.

In 1934 Portsmouth's opponents were Manchester City, who had finished fifth in the League. (Portsmouth finished tenth.) The names of two of the Manchester team will be familiar to all football followers. Goalkeeper Frank Swift played many times for England, and right-half Matt Busby became Manchester United's manager and was knighted for his services to football. At half-time Portsmouth were a goal up but in the second half made the mistake of concentrating on defence to hold on to their slender lead. Manchester equalised while one of the Portsmouth players was off the field injured and scored the winning goal three minutes from time.

So in 1939 Portsmouth were trying for the third time to win the elusive trophy. Both teams had been drawn at home in all of the rounds up to the semifinals, a decided advantage for any team but especially so for Portsmouth who had an indifferent season in the First Division, eventually finishing 17th only five points clear of relegation. Wolves on the other hand had finished second in the table behind Everton. Portsmouth, in reaching the final, had conceded only one goal to Wolves' three (but had scored only eleven to Wolves' 19).

The official attendance at Wembley in 1939 was 99,370, the largest crowd since 1923. Of these about 13,000-14,000 were Portsmouth supporters. Many thousands arrived from Portsmouth by special excursion train, about 2,000 by coach and 2,000 by private car and taxi.

Two weeks before the final, a protest meeting organized

by the Portsmouth Football Supporters' Club, attended by more than 2,000 people, had demanded the appointment of a commission to inquire into the distribution of Cup Final tickets. The secretary of the club said that of the 24,000 who regularly attended Portsmouth's games not more than 1,000 had managed to obtain tickets from a direct source. The Supporters' Club had not been granted any tickets, its members having had to take their chance with the general public. About 5,000 tickets had been sold at the ground and the directors had disposed of an unknown number. About 7,000 tickets remained unaccounted for.

Wolves were odds-on favourites to win because of the form they had shown throughout the season. Their captain, Stan Cullis, the England international centre-half, felt confident that his team would win. He was the only Wolves player to have previously appeared at Wembley (when he played for England). Major Frank Buckley, the Wolves manager, said that the result was not a foregone conclusion but thought that his team could play well enough to beat Portsmouth.

The Portsmouth team, after training all week at Bognor Regis, had gone to Wembley to inspect the ground. Only one of their players, outside-right Worrall, had played in Portsmouth's previous final there in 1934. Their manager, Jack Tinn, famous for the spats he wore, was confident. 'I do think we shall win the Cup,' he said. Their captain, Jimmy Guthrie, after being presented with a lucky horseshoe, said, 'With that and the manager's spats the Cup is in the bag.' Both teams made history by receiving mysterious 'gland' treatment before the match. Whether this was the equivalent of today's forbidden drugs is not known but it seemed to have a more beneficial effect on one team than on the other.

If the Cup Final had been held a month or two earlier Wolves would have been even more overwhelming favourites. In the last few weeks, however, they had fallen out of the championship race and had perhaps lost a little of that self-confidence and attacking flair that had promised to land them the Cup and League double. Portsmouth on the other hand had escaped from their dangerous relegation position by picking up a few precious points and their forwards were finding the net once again.

The strength of the Wolves team lay in their attacking half-back line of Galley, Cullis and Gardiner, who were adept at providing their forwards with a steady stream of passes. The speed and accuracy of the Wolves forwards, especially centre-forward Westcott, was well known and it was expected that the game would develop into a contest for supremacy between the Wolves forwards and the Portsmouth defence.

Portsmouth for their part had a solid defence and the pick of their forwards were Worrall and Barlow. The latter by a strange twist of fate had been transferred from Wolves only that very season. *The Times* predicted that the final would be the usual exciting mixture of good and bad football with Wolves the winners at the end. In comparison with today's financial incentives it is worth noting that the members of the Portsmouth team would each receive £12 as a bonus if they won! The teams were:

PORTSMOUTH
Walker

	Morgan			Rochford	
	Guthrie		Rowe		Wharton
Worrall	McAlinden		Anderson	Barlow	Parker

WOLVERHAMPTON
Scott

	Morris			Taylor	
	Galley		Cullis		Gardiner
Burton	McIntosh		Westcott	Dorsett	Maguire

117

Pompey's glory – heroes of the 1939 Cup Final. L to r standing: Stewart (trainer), Anderson, Morgan, Rowe, Walker, Rochford, Wharton, Tinn (manager). Seated: Worrall, McAlinden, Guthrie, Barlow, Parker.

On Cup Final day a strong wind was blowing straight across the pitch and a shower of rain fell about an hour before the kick-off. The pitch was firm but not hard. The King and Queen arrived just before 3 pm and the two teams, already lined up, were presented to the King by the two captains.

Guthrie won the toss and had choice of ends. In the very first minute Portsmouth conceded a corner when Walker turned a shot round the post. The goalkeeper punched the corner-kick away and Portsmouth then conceded a free kick near the half-way line from which Westcott received the ball and shot a couple of yards wide. These two incidents apart, nearly all the action in the first ten minutes took place in the Wolves half and their defence was frequently in difficulties.

Five minutes after the start Portsmouth could have scored. A right-wing cross to Anderson was intercepted and passed back to Scott, but Anderson dashed in and dispossessed the goalkeeper, who had left his goal. The ball ran to Worrall but when he centred it Scott had scrambled back and was able to clear it. After one Portsmouth attack an appeal for a penalty for hands was ignored by the referee.

So right from the start of the game any thoughts of a Wolves walk-over were quickly dispelled. The Portsmouth half-back line soon asserted itself and of the two teams Portsmouth began to play the more methodical football. In defence the two backs and Walker in goal gave nothing away. Barlow at inside-left inspired the other forwards with his astute passing, while Worrall's speed was proving a constant danger to the Wolves defence. Cullis, the Wolves centre-half, was strangely uncertain of himself early on.

Wolves' most dangerous attack came after 20 minutes when Dorsett unleashed a drive that Walker turned round the post. This effort apart, all the excitement was at the other end with Wolves defending desperately at times against constant Portsmouth attacks. After 25 minutes the pressure was relieved for a time when Wolves broke away and forced two corners.

In the 31st minute Anderson, in the inside-right position, beat Cullis to the ball and nodded it on to the unmarked Barlow, who found plenty of time to steady himself and drive it into the net with Scott helpless to save. A second goal for Portsmouth came just before the interval. A shot from Anderson was blocked but he managed to regain possession of the ball and fire it into the goal. Scott, who seemed to misjudge the angle, got his fingers to the ball but could not prevent it from going over the line.

In the first minute of the second half Portsmouth scored a third goal. Parker and Barlow raced down the pitch passing the ball from one to the other. Barlow's shot should have been saved by Scott, who made a frantic grab for the ball while lying on the ground. There was some doubt whether the ball was over the line at that point but Parker raced up and helped it into the back of the net to make sure. The balance of opinion seemed to be that Scott was holding the ball exactly on the goal-line when Parker applied the finishing touch. Parker himself gave that version of the incident afterwards.

All praise from then on went to Wolves who refused to let the score discourage them with Cullis trying his hardest to rally his team. Seven minutes into the half their efforts resulted in a consolation goal when Dorsett fired in a splendid shot that gave Walker no chance. Had Portsmouth faltered at that point there might have been a remarkable ending to the match but they pulled themselves together and resumed their masterly display of the first half. They seemed to go from strength to strength and finally added a fourth goal, perhaps the best of the match. Worrall sped down the wing with the ball and from his centre Parker headed it into the net like a bullet.

Portsmouth had won on their merits after a decisive and brilliant display of football. Right from the start they had looked the more confident side and the longer the game went on so Portsmouth showed their superiority, playing with calmness and authority. The quick, strong tackling of their half-back line threw the Wolves forwards out of their stride, not allowing them to practise their usual smooth rhythmic passing of the ball. Throughout the game Portsmouth played the better-balanced and more methodical football. Each man marked his opponent closely, and the two backs covered each other and the goalkeeper with near-perfect understanding. Barlow's clever passes continually opened gaps in the Wolves defence and Worrall's speed and footwork proved a constant menace.

Wolves lacked inspiration and they were never really the masters of their nerves. Cullis's uncertainty in the first half unsettled their defence, which was too often drawn out of

120

position, leaving wide gaps for the Portsmouth forwards to exploit. The Wolves half-back line, usually a tower of strength, found itself too hard pressed to give the forwards the service of the ball to which they were accustomed. The forwards themselves were often ineffective and nothing like as dangerous on the ball as the Portsmouth forwards.

When all is said and done a team plays as well as it is allowed to do, and Portsmouth did not allow Wolves to play their usual game. It must have been frustrating for Wolves to find such calm and confident opponents. Once again the Cup favourites had come to grief, perhaps through over-confidence, although Portsmouth supporters always maintained that the result reflected the superior skills and ability of the Portsmouth team. Nobody could deny that on the day they made Wolves look like a second-rate side.

The Portsmouth team returned home that same evening by train from Waterloo with the Cup, the first time it had ever travelled south of London. A vast crowd met them at Portsmouth and it took an hour for their coach to travel the short distance from the railway station to the Guildhall. There speeches were delivered by the Lord Mayor, the Bishop of Portsmouth, the chairman of directors, the manager and the captain. The chairman of directors said that he hoped to see different arrangements for the distribution of tickets next time. To date there has not been a 'next time' as Portsmouth have not appeared at Wembley in a Cup Final since that glorious day in 1939. They came closest in 1992 when they lost to Liverpool in a semifinal replay after a penalty 'shoot-out'.

Bibliography

★

The following books were used for reference:

Chapter
1   Hobsbawm E J & Rudé G *Captain Swing* Lawrence and Wishart 1969
       Hammond J L *The Village Labourer* Longmans 1966
2   Anstruther I *The Scandal of the Andover Workhouse* Bles 1973
       Crowther M A *The Workhouse System 1834-1929* Univ. of Georgia Press 1982
3   Lloyd A *The Great Prize Fight* Cassell 1977
8   Barton M E *An Engineering Geological Appraisal of the Foundations and Underpinning of Winchester Cathedral* Balkema 1988
       Henderson I & Crook J *The Winchester Diver* Henderson and Stirk 1984
9   Barker R *The Schneider Trophy Races* Chatto and Windus 1971
11   Brode A *The Southampton Blitz* B Shurlock 1977
       Frankland, Hyslop & Jemima *Southampton Blitz: The Unofficial Story* Southampton Local Studies 1990
       Rance A *Southampton: An Illustrated History* Milestone 1986
12   Robertson A J *The Bleak Midwinter* Manchester Univ. Press 1987
14   Hutton J B *Commander Crabb is Alive* Tandem 1968
15   Neasom, Cooper & Robinson *Pompey : The History of Portsmouth Football Club* Milestone 1984

The following newspapers were used for reference:
Aldershot News, Farnborough Times, Hampshire Advertiser, Hampshire Chronicle, Hampshire Independent, Hampshire Observer, Hants and Berks Gazette, Portsmouth Evening News, Portsmouth (now *Hampshire*) *Telegraph, Southern Daily* (now *Evening*) *Echo, The Daily Telegraph*, and *The Times.*

Index